You have only to dip into this astounding memoir to see that the suffering that marked Nonna's early years was the very thing that God used to shape this remarkable woman. Denise George and Carolyn Tomlin have managed to give Nonna Bannister the same feeling of literary and historical importance that John and Elizabeth Sherrill brought to Corrie ten Boom in *The Hiding Place*. Read it and weep or read it and rejoice, but above all, read it.

CALVIN MILLER
PROFESSOR OF DIVINITY, BEESON DIVINITY SCHOOL

What a marvelous service has been provided by Denise George and Carolyn Tomlin in bringing to light the untold story of Nonna Bannister! This inspiring volume provides a window into the personal and painful reflections of one of the darkest periods in human history. Yet readers will be strengthened by reading this most moving and hopeful account of courage, faith, and forgiveness.

DAVID S. DOCKERY
PRESIDENT, UNION UNIVERSITY

This book is absolutely captivating. It is an extraordinary glimpse inside the oppressive nature of Russian Communism and the viciously evil heart of Nazi Germany. But, the revelations of human depravity manifested in horrific acts of brutality and murder notwithstanding, rays of God's Light appear in the form of a Russian Orthodox grandmother, a frail Jewish boy, and a group of Christlike German Catholic nuns and priests. These diaries are at once heartbreaking, hopeful, and unforgettable.

LYLE W. DORSETT
BILLY GRAHAM PROFESSOR OF EVANGELISM
BEESON DIVINITY SCHOOL

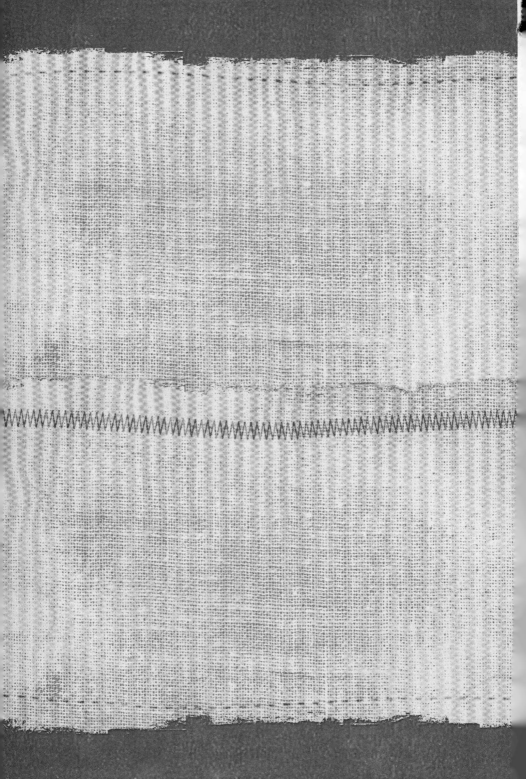

THE SECRET HOLOCAUST DIARIES

NONNA BANNISTER

WITH DENISE GEORGE
AND CAROLYN TOMLIN

TYNDALE HOUSE PUBLISHERS, INC.
CAROL STREAM, ILLINOIS

the secret
HOLOCAUST DIARIES

The untold story of Nonna Bannister

Visit Tyndale online at www.tyndale.com.

TYNDALE and Tyndale's quill logo are registered trademarks of Tyndale House Publishers, Inc.

The Secret Holocaust Diaries: The Untold Story of Nonna Bannister

Copyright © 2009 by NLB Partners. All rights reserved.

Cover and interior photos are used by permission from the Nonna Bannister family collection.

Designed by Jacqueline L. Nuñez

Published in association with the literary agency of WordServe Literary Group, Inc., 10152 Knoll Circle, Highlands Ranch, CO 80130.

Library of Congress Cataloging-in-Publication Data

Bannister, Nonna, 1927-2004.
   The secret Holocaust diaries : the untold story of Nonna Bannister / by Nonna Bannister ; with Carolyn Tomlin and Denise George.
    p. cm.
  ISBN 978-1-4143-2546-0 (hc)
  ISBN 978-1-4143-2547-7 (sc)
1. Bannister, Nonna, 1927-2004. 2. World war, 1939-1945—Women—Ukraine—Kostiantynivka (Donetska oblast)—Biography. 3. World war, 1939-1945—Children—Ukraine—Kostiantynivka (Donetska oblast)—Biography. 4. World War, 1939-1945—Prisoners and prisons, German. 5. Holocaust, Jewish (1939-1945)—Ukraine. 6. Kostiantynivka (Donetska oblast, Ukraine)—Biography. I. Tomlin, Carolyn Ross. II. George, Denise. III. Title.
  DK508.835.B36A3 2009
  940.53′18092—dc22
  [B]   2008050099

Printed in the United States of America

20   19   18   17   16   15
21   20   19   18   17   16

Dedication
circa 1990

I would like to dedicate this book to the memory of all those who perished during the Holocaust in World War II, who are no longer here to tell their stories, and also to those who survived the horrors of it all but lost their families and loved ones.

I thank God for the little Jewish boy named Nathan, who died so that I could live.

I want to express my gratitude to the Catholic priests and nuns who were brave enough to hide me from the Gestapo after they had taken my mother away.

I want to express my deepest gratitude to my loving and caring husband, Henry, who has given me his support and his understanding and caring for me—for sharing my feelings with me and helping me throughout our forty-six years of marriage to cope with the many sad memories of the past. I feel that God sent him to me because He knew what I needed to survive the many hard times. Henry took care of me while I struggled through very bad health, and without him and his love and support, it would have been extremely difficult to write this book and to cope with so many horrible memories.

I thank God for giving me three beautiful children—two sons: W. H. (Hank) Jr. and John D., and a beautiful daughter, Elizabeth J. They also have given me a lot of support and love, which I will cherish until I die.

Nonna L. Bannister

TO THE PAST

To the past, the way has been barred,
And what do I need the past for now?
What is there? Bloodied flagstone—
Or a bricked-up door—or an echo
That still cannot die away . . .
However much I beg.

Nonna L. Bannister

Contents

Preface

This is the true story of a Russian-American woman named Nonna Lisowskaja Bannister.

The material within these pages comes from the private, handwritten transcripts that Nonna made of her diaries from childhood, World War II, and the years immediately following the war. She expanded and compiled them during the late 1980s, with further commentary based on her memory of events. Translating into English from her original documents, which were written in five languages, Nonna wrote her life story on yellow legal pads and kept them hidden from everyone, including her husband, Henry.

In the 1990s, after decades of marriage, Nonna finally told Henry about her secret past. She also made him promise that he wouldn't share any of her hidden material until after her death. Henry kept his promise to Nonna, only now making her writings public after her death in 2004.

Nonna had kept a lifetime of secret diaries. She began writing as a young girl and received a diary of her own from her father when she was nine years old. In this childhood diary she described her life, her family, and her dreams, and she included some of her poetry. She also kept a formal diary during the latter years of World War II, when Catholic nuns at a German hospital hid her from the Nazis and nursed her back to health. She continued this diary in the years immediately following the war.

During World War II, when Nonna left the Ukraine and traveled to Nazi Germany, she kept a pillow made of black and white ticking tied around her waist. In this small pillow, she kept her thin childhood diary, various bundles of paper scraps on which she kept notes of her wartime experiences, and several photographs and family documents. In addition to the written record that Nonna left of her memories—transcribed onto pads of paper and then typed by Henry Bannister—the Bannister family has in its possession one of Nonna's diaries, dated 1947–48; postcards from Nonna's mother, dated 1944–45; and many other personal documents and photographs from the Word War II era.

Fluent in at least seven languages, Nonna did the translation work herself. She transcribed her diaries from the various languages in which she had written them into English, one of the last languages she learned—which may account for some of the awkwardness of English grammar and sentence construction in her memoir. Also, transcribing the diaries years after the events described in them and adding her own present-day commentary in places, she did not always adhere to a linear progression. Thus, though translation was not necessary, some minor editing was. Efforts were also made to bring Nonna's family names to a consistent spelling, though it was not possible to maintain any one style of transliteration.

The editors have in some cases combined into one place events that Nonna recorded in different places in her transcripts, as well as giving explanation to the historical chronology in the appendix. Throughout her text, editorial comments have been added where an explanation seemed helpful for better understanding of the transcripts, the historical settings, and Nonna's family. Some of this commentary comes from Henry Bannister's remembrances of Nonna's stories.

Though similar to other memoirs of the war and the Holocaust years, Nonna's account provides a rare glimpse into the life of a girl who was born to a wealthy family in the Ukraine, experienced great suffering in Stalin's Soviet Union, and eventually lost her family and her own freedom at the hands of Nazi Germany. It is a story with unusual significance as one of the few firsthand accounts of a girl from a once-privileged family, who fell into the ranks of the *Ostarbeiter*—the primarily Ukrainian "Eastern laborers" transported to Germany during the war as slave labor under Adolf Hitler's regime. The fact that she not only survived such turmoil and tragedy but also moved on through faith in God to forgive those who took away so much makes her story all the more remarkable.

Carolyn Tomlin
Jackson, Tennessee

Denise George
Birmingham, Alabama
Summer 2008

Introduction

I have now decided that the time has come when I must share my life story—not only with my loving family, but perhaps with all those who are interested to know what life was like for many of us on the other side of the world before and during World War II. I wish to speak the truth and nothing but the truth—but some things I shall keep to myself—nobody needs them but me. I doubt that anyone reveals the whole truth about oneself, even in confession. There are things in everyone's life that are known only to oneself and our almighty Father God.

The events described in the following pages were written from my diaries and notes that were transcribed from the four to six languages in which I had written them—starting when I was nine years old. I have translated the poems and thoughts and scripts into English. I have worked on keeping these all together since 1942, when Mama and I left our homeland and were sent to Germany, where we were to be slave labor. In these notes, I kept a record of all the terrors, atrocities, and the new life into which we were thrown. Throughout these ordeals, I never forgot my grandmother and the rest of my family, which had been torn apart and ultimately destroyed—when I would hear a train whistle in the distance, I would immediately think that my dear brother, Anatoly, would be on that train and on his way back to us. This work is an effort to tell the truth about what took place during World War II under the direction of Hitler and his Gestapo troops.

There are not many of us remaining that lived through those very difficult and troubled times and are now free to tell the true stories of life. Many, including my own family, perished before having a chance to reach freedom. I am compelled to write this story because I was a witness to many events that took place then and because I am the only survivor of my entire family.

I do regret that I did not write this story sooner. But when I came to America in June of 1950, I was overwhelmed by my new life. I wanted so much to forget the unhappiness of the past and to make a new and happy life for myself that I actually shut the door to the past and had no desire to dwell on it. And a happy life I have made for myself by falling in love with the most kind and wonderful man and marrying him on June 23, 1951.

When my first son, "Hank," was born on October 30, 1953, there was just no end to my happiness. I engrossed myself completely in motherhood, and I loved my husband and my son too much to ever even think of my sad past. So I became a wife and a mother full time. Then my daughter, Elizabeth, was born on July 11, 1957, and my happiness and duties as a full-time mother increased. My youngest son, John, was born on March 27, 1959, which happened to be on Good Friday of that year. My family became my only concern, and my entire interest was now directed exclusively to my husband and my children. I was filled with love and the responsibilities of taking care of them and loving them with all my heart and mind.

There were times when I would think about my family that I had lost, and I would think about how close and loving we had been. However, I just could not bring myself to inflict my sad memories on my husband and my still-young children. I did not want anything to interfere with the happiness that we had, and certainly when the children were growing up, my only concern was to protect them from anything that would leave them with depressing impressions. I wanted so very much to create a healthy and happy environment for all of them.

Now that the children have grown up and are well-adjusted and intelligent human beings, I feel that they should know more about their ancestors from my side of the family—that my children must know how they lived and how they died. I also feel that by telling my true life story, I may be revealing some facts from the past that could make a contribution, however small it may be, to the history of mankind.

It is very difficult for me to relive that part of my life even through the memories that are still with me—so precise and vivid. However, I have an uncontrollable desire to write about those years of my life, which were filled not only with sad events but also with happy times when I was growing up and still had all my family. It took great effort to put my story together, but I have had tremendous support from my loving husband. I feel very fortunate to have had him by my side and to have his encouragement. Without this encouragement, it would have been very difficult to go through with it.

When I left Russia, I took with me a passionate love for my homeland the way it was before the Bolshevik Revolution— the Russia I knew from the stories that were told to me by my dear grandmother and my loving parents. My hope and desire is to live long enough to see my homeland, the country so dear to me, become free again as it was before I was born. The hope that I live with and my prayers to God are that I will see—or at least my children and grandchildren will see—Russia become the "Old Mother *Rossija*" as it used to be—to see Russia return to its beauty and magnificence.

Is it really possible for this to ever happen again? "The Rossija shall become free again"—those were the words of my dear grandmother. It was a promise that she made to us, her grandchildren, as well as to her children. The beautiful land where creativity, art, and music would flourish again someday, free and independent. The land where the Russian people would be able to exercise their talents freely.

I get furiously angry at the thought of what has been done to my ancestors and to the land I love so much. But I do feel very fortunate to have at least some knowledge, which was passed on to me by my own family before I lost them. I shall try to pass this on to my own children so that they will know the truth and be as proud of their roots as I am.

How can one tell the story, especially *write* the story, without knowledge of the writer? The story is so real and so full of horrors. How can I describe the things that I have seen and felt and that made me the sole survivor of my family—all the troubled times and horrors and terror that surrounded all of us? It is difficult for me to put my thoughts into proper perspective, especially since my English vocabulary is somewhat limited.

Though I have lived in America for forty-seven years, I still find it difficult to express my thoughts properly. I have yet another problem, which is that I have allowed myself to forget the languages I knew so well when I came to this country. I spoke six languages very well, and most of my notes and some of my poems, which I wrote between nine years old and nineteen years old, were written in the Russian, Ukrainian, Polish, Latvian, and German languages.

I kept diaries during those years, and even as I lay in the hospital stricken with rheumatic fever and the ensuing heart problems, I continued to write in my diary for some time before I left Germany. My diary was written in several languages, but it was written with the deep feelings of one who had gone through a great deal of sad times. Most of my writings were about my mother, father, and my brother, Anatoly. I also became very close to God Himself, and my writings were full of expressed feelings toward faith in God and His mercy on me. I felt very close to God, and I felt that He had chosen to keep me alive for a very definite purpose. So I put into writing all my feelings—as best I could—and all that I had learned about God from my dear grandmother and my parents.

Translating from my own notes and diaries, I find myself in a great state of confusion, because it is difficult for me—after so many years—to understand my own writing, especially since the languages it was all written in became somewhat estranged to me. However, with extra time and much effort, it finally comes to me, and I am able to put it into English so that at least I can understand the meaning of my own thoughts during those troubled times. When I wrote some of my poems, I wrote them under the influence of grief, which was still with me after losing my entire family. It was so recent, and I was still in shock from the whole ordeal.

My age has become a hindrance to me in remembering some of the events that took place during the very early part of my childhood. But it seems that I manage to block out the sad times in my memory and to concentrate only on the happy ones. Little by little, all of it comes back to me as though by chain reaction. It may take me some time to put it all together, but I am so inspired to write that I don't think anything can prevent or discourage me from writing my true life story now. I only wish that I had some education in writing stories, even if it is the story of my own life.

Perhaps someday I will be able to put it all in proper perspective, but right now I only want to get it out of my head and just write it down the best I know how. What I write is all true, and I have witnessed all of it. Most of all, I like to write about things that I learned from my grandmother and my loving parents.

Nonna L. Bannister

Prologue

Henry Bannister met Nonna Lisowskaja in 1951. He knew little about her when she agreed to marry him. She was a mysterious woman with a painful secret—a secret she hid from him for more than forty years of marriage.

A decade before Nonna died, she took him by the hand and led him to the attic of their small house in Memphis, Tennessee.

"It's time," she said.

Henry had waited a long while for those words. He didn't know what secrets the attic held, but he had watched his wife climb those stairs many times, disappearing into the night for some unknown reason. He never asked why she went or what she did up there, knowing that she could not speak about it and deeply respecting her privacy.

He also never inquired about the black-and-white-striped ticking pillow Nonna held to her heart each night at bedtime. He just knew she couldn't sleep without it.

Nor did Henry ask Nonna about her family back in Germany or Russia, or wherever she had come from. He knew she'd tell him when she was ready. So he waited.

Only once did Nonna give Henry a glimpse into her painful past. They and their three young children attended a church service at Central Baptist Church in Baton Rouge, Louisiana, at which the guest speaker told of his harrowing Holocaust experiences at the hands of German Nazis. Nonna shocked Henry by jumping up from the pew and running out of the sanctuary, crying. He quietly gathered the children and took Nonna home. She immediately went to bed—and stayed there for several weeks. Henry didn't know how to help her.

"What's wrong, Mama?" their younger son, John, asked again and again. "Mama, what's wrong?" John received a mother's embrace, but no answer to his question.

Again, Henry didn't pry into Nonna's past. He simply took care of the house and children, and he waited for her to get up from her bed, to reveal what had so disturbed her.

Many years later, he was still waiting. The children had grown up, married, and built lives of their own. Nonna suffered with her health—her heart and her back—and underwent several surgeries. Her fingers knotted with painful arthritis, Henry's eyesight dimmed, and together they grew old. Then one day, out of the blue, she spoke the words he longed to hear: "Henry, it's time."

They climbed the attic stairs and sat down beside the old heavy wooden trunk Nonna had painted lime-green—the color of living things. She picked up a worn key and turned the metal lock. She showed Henry old photographs, introducing him one by one to her family: grandmother, aunts and uncles, mother and father, cousins, friends—all of them dead, long buried a world away in unmarked graves. The last photograph Nonna pulled from the trunk was one of her only sibling, Anatoly.

"He'd be almost seventy years old now," she said.

Nonna reached into the trunk. She took from it a fragile, hand-sewn diary, its pages filled with writing in Russian.

"My childhood diary," she said. "Papa gave it to me on my ninth birthday."

Then she put into Henry's hands a small pad of paper—diaries she had written immediately after the war, each page covered with microscopic pencil marks.

He held the small pad of paper up to the attic's ceiling bulb and tried to read the faded words.

"My eyes are too weak to read them, Nonna. What do they say?"

"They're hard to read, Henry. I wrote in such tiny print."

"How am I to learn your secrets, Nonna, if I can't read your diaries?"

Nonna smiled. Then, from the trunk she pulled a thick stack of legal pads, each long yellow page filled with hand-penned words.

"The translations of my diaries, and my story," she said. "In English."

Then Nonna climbed down the attic stairs, and Henry began to read.

Train to Agony

CHAPTER 1

BOARDING THE TRAIN

August 7, 1942—Konstantinowka, Ukraine

It is fourteen hours and fifteen minutes (2:15 p.m.), and we were just loaded on the train! My God—this is not what we thought it would be like to make this journey! We are packed like sardines in a can into the cattle cars of the train. The German soldiers with their rifles are with us and Mama is scared. (I know that she is.) Mama still thinks we can get off the train and leave our luggage behind and walk home. There is Grandmother standing about twenty feet away, looking so shocked and in dismay—she is crying—with the tears running down her face as she waves good-bye. Somehow, I know that we will never see her again.

As the train starts to move, Mama and I just look at

Grandmother until she is out of sight. At the hour of 1600 (4:00 p.m.) everyone inside our car is very quiet and nobody is talking. Some are crying quietly—and I am glad that I have my diary and two pencils.

I got into the corner as far as I could so I would have some room to write. Now the door of our car is open, but I can hear some noises from the top of the roof. The German soldiers had positioned themselves on the top of the train, and they are talking and singing—I think they are drinking—they sound drunk to me.

It is almost midnight—the moon is so full—and we are crossing large fields. I need to get closer to the door so I can get some fresh air. As I approach the open door, I see a pair of legs in black boots dangling right above the door—then this face leans down and the soldier yells, "Hi, pretty one!" and I get away from the door very quickly. Mama pulls me closer to herself, and I think I am getting sleepy.

August 8, 1942

When we wake up, we can look into the horizon and see the sun rising from the edges of the biggest fields that I have ever seen—it is a beautiful sunrise! Where are we? How close are we to Kiev? The train is slowing down, and it looks as though we will stop moving.

August 9, 1942

We are in Kiev, but the train stopped at least a block away from the large train station. The Germans jumped down, and I could see how many of them there were—we were surrounded. They were telling us to get out—"*Raus, raus.*" We saw trucks approaching the train, loaded with German soldiers and

German shepherd dogs (lots of dogs). There was a truck loaded with food (soup made with cabbage and potatoes, and there was black bread). They passed out some bowls to us, and as we walked to the food truck, I looked to the back of the train and I saw two cars loaded with Jews. They were not allowed to get out—the doors of their cars were barred with heavy metal bars, and the German soldiers were guarding them. I saw old men, women, children, and even some babies. They were begging us to give them some of our bread with their thin (almost skeletonlike) hands stuck out through the bars. I started to go there with my food, but just as I got close to them, a German soldier shouted at me and commanded me to get back or he would shoot me if I dared come any closer.

SEPARATE CARS • The Jewish prisoners, headed for concentration "death" camps, were in the same transport but rode in separate train cars from the Russian women, who were headed for the labor camps. The Nazis allowed the Russian women to leave their cars, go into the woods to relieve themselves, and eat. But they allowed no such privileges to the Jews.

August 9, 1942—late evening

When we got back into the car of the train (Car 8) and the train started to move, we thought that we were on the way again. But in fifteen minutes, our train came to a stop. Three trucks loaded with Jews approached our train, and the Germans loaded them into the first two cars of our train. It was close enough for us to hear the screams of the children, the wailings and moaning of the women. There were shots fired frequently. Oh! Those screams and cries! And the dogs—there were so many of them. It was mass confusion, and I became aware that we, too, were prisoners and that there was absolutely no way to escape as Mama had planned to do when we got to Kiev.

August 10, 1942

We are leaving the Ukraine now, and the train is moving fast. I will never forget the sight of the last sunset as we were leaving Kiev. The sun looked like a huge ball of red and orange fire, and it was moving down slowly against the horizon at the end of the endless fields. Almost it was as though the sun were saying, "Farewell, my dear—we shall never meet on this soil again!" As I stood there near the door of our train car, I kept looking at the sun until it had completely disappeared. Then I suddenly felt very sad and lonely. It was a "farewell" that made me feel that a part of me had died. Many sunsets and sunrises were thereafter, but never was one so beautiful as the sunset that I saw at Kiev.

"MANY . . . WERE THEREAFTER" • In some places it is difficult to distinguish what Nonna might have written during or just after the war from what she added later to her transcript. In this chapter, Nonna directly translates her diaries almost exclusively, though this comment reflects her backward look at this story from a late-twentieth-century point of view.

Now I know that we are heading into Poland, and Mama is beginning to make plans for us to escape when we make the first stop in Poland. The next stop is for a meal. We will crawl under the car and wait for everyone to get loaded, and we will get out quickly and run toward the wooded area. Mama is planning.

CHAPTER 2

BABY SARAH

*This horrible story, which I blocked out of
my mind for so many years, suddenly comes
back to me along with other memories that
now surface one by one.*

On August 11, 1942, we were in Poland, and our train made
a stop for us to use the woods nearby. There was another train,
which was heading in the opposite direction, stopped on the
adjacent tracks. The train was loaded with Jews heading for
one of the extermination camps. The people were so pitiful;
they were dressed in rags and looked as if they had not seen
food for such a long time. Some of them looked like human

skeletons—they were so thin that they looked like death! The SS men and the German soldiers had unloaded all the people from our train to go into the bushes to use the bathroom. The German soldiers were standing guard with many dogs with them, which they would use to chase down anyone who tried to escape. These dogs had been trained to attack and kill upon the command of the soldiers.

After the Germans had reloaded the people onto our train, everyone was looking at the train loaded with the Jewish prisoners. It was so sad to see the condition of these people. Our train started to move very slowly. I was glad to be moving, because what I had just seen made me feel very sick to my stomach. The Jews did not look like humans but, rather, like skeletons covered with a greenish-gray-colored skin; their eyes seemed to be very big, and they were staring at us. Thin—very thin—hands were stretched out toward our car, begging for food, and the people were making sounds barely above a whisper. There were little hands of small children, and old hands of old men and women, begging for bread or anything to eat. On the side of the cars, which were packed like sardines with these Jewish people, there were yellow Jewish stars painted very sloppily—you could sense that these stars had been painted with much hate and disgust.

"TO USE THE BATHROOM" • This American euphemism is another example of Nonna's occasional anachronistic comments throughout her diary transcripts—as is her "packed like sardines," and her use of the postwar term *extermination camp*. Her diaries were written as the events took place, but by the time she translated and expanded them, she had been a citizen of the United States for many years.

Mama and I had placed ourselves closer to the open door of our train car, hoping to get some fresh air. Suddenly there was a young girl running alongside our car—no one knew where she had come from. She had a look of terror in her eyes, and she had her arms around a small bundle. Her black hair was blowing in the wind, and she was so thin that you could see her bones protruding from her neck and her shoulders. She hurled her bundle at Mama, and before any of us realized what happened, Mama stood there holding the bundle in her hands—and we heard a baby cry! The young woman was still running alongside our train car. She yelled out, "Please, oh please, save my baby—please give her a Russian name!"

By then, the train had begun to move faster, but we could see the girl still standing by the tracks with her hands covering her face, and she was weeping. The rest of the women in our rail car surrounded Mama and me as we stood there in disbelief and shock, watching the baby. It all happened so fast that it took a little while to realize what had just happened.

For hours, there were all kinds of insults exchanged among the women. Some of the women were on Mama's side and decided to come up with some story to tell the Germans as to how the baby got there—"We can tell the Germans that when we returned to our car, the baby was already here"—and hide the true story that the baby was thrown to us by a Jewish girl. There were some who suggested that we tell the Germans that a Polish woman had left the baby with us and asked us to take the baby to Germany. It was obvious to all of us that we had to hide the fact that the baby was Jewish. It was the only way to save the baby. It went on for hours as our train kept moving on, and we knew that we would soon be approaching the German border.

Some of the women were emotionally moved by having a part in saving the baby's life. But there were some of the women that did not want to take part because it might jeopardize them. We could all be punished for what we were trying to do and even be transferred to the Jewish trains, which were headed for the concentration camps. There would not be any escape if that happened, and no one really knew what would happen as soon as the Germans found the baby. There was no possible way that someone on our train could have had this baby, since we were extensively screened prior to being loaded on the trains. We had all gone through these medical screenings.

The women began to take turns holding the baby, and we began to call her Sarah. But Mama still insisted that we call her Taissia, which was my baby sister's name. She had died when she was only three days old. *Taissia* was a Russian name, and the baby would have a better chance to survive if she had a Russian name rather than being called Sarah.

The baby was crying, and we knew that we had to find some way to feed her, but there was absolutely no way. We had no milk or anything to put liquids of any kind into. Some of the women tried to nurse the baby, but it was impossible. We thought that if we could keep the baby quiet until the next train stop, one of us could take her to the wooded area close to a road, and leave her there with a note written in Polish, making it look like some Polish woman had abandoned her. Then perhaps some Polish people would find the baby and adopt her, or at least take care of her. Everyone was trying to think of some idea to handle this situation.

"WE HAD NO MILK" • The Germans required qualified women workers to be between ages 16 and 35, and though infants were not allowed, it was certainly possible that some women had recently given birth and might still be able to nurse.

However, there was a young woman in our car who absolutely refused to go along with any of it. Her name was Dunja—she was from the same town that Mama and I were from. She kept saying that she would tell the Germans about the whole thing and that no way would she take part in protecting or saving a *zydowka* (a Jew girl), even if she was just a baby. She would not agree to our ideas—the only one she wanted to save was herself. Of course, everyone was worried about her—especially Mama, since Dunja had directed all her threats toward Mama.

Suddenly, when we did not expect it, our train began to slow down in the middle of the fields, and the train was coming to a stop. The baby was crying, and we were all absolutely terrified. The German soldiers jumped out of the cars ahead and rushed to all the cars yelling, "*Raus! Raus!*" There was a truckload of German soldiers near the track ahead, and we knew immediately that these were SS men. I tried to listen to the Germans and figure out what they were saying so I could know what was going on.

It seemed that we were coming closer to German land, and this was an inspection of all the train cars and occupants. The Germans wanted to make sure that there were no Jews smuggled out of Poland. I looked back and saw Mama holding baby "Sarah" in her arms, and terror struck me all over again. *What happens now?* But we didn't have to wait long to find out, as the baby let out a cry, and the German soldier that had ordered us out of the rail car looked at us with disbelief.

Before anyone could say anything, Dunja yelled, "It's a baby Jew—the Jewish woman threw it into our car at the last stop!" She could not say it in German very well, but it was good enough for the German soldier to understand. He motioned for other soldiers, and they rushed toward us. Mama held onto the baby very tightly and would not let go as the German soldier tried to take her. I started to beg Mama to give the baby to him before he used force. Finally another soldier grabbed Mama by her shoulders, and the German soldier took the baby.

The soldier handed the baby to an SS man who carried the baby away—holding her body in his one hand, and letting it hang down by his side. Mama broke into tears, and with terror in my heart, I watched the SS man carry the infant to the truck. He raised up one of his knees and with a swift motion brought the baby's body down against his knee.

I no longer heard the baby cry, and when I tried to move, I could not. I felt the blood leaving my head, and I was feeling sick and dizzy. When I came to, I was standing by the door of the rail car, throwing up violently. Mama was kneeling beside me, and she was saying over and over again, "They killed my Taissia, my sweet baby!" I realized that she was still in shock, and I put my arms around her and held her very tightly.

Life Before the War

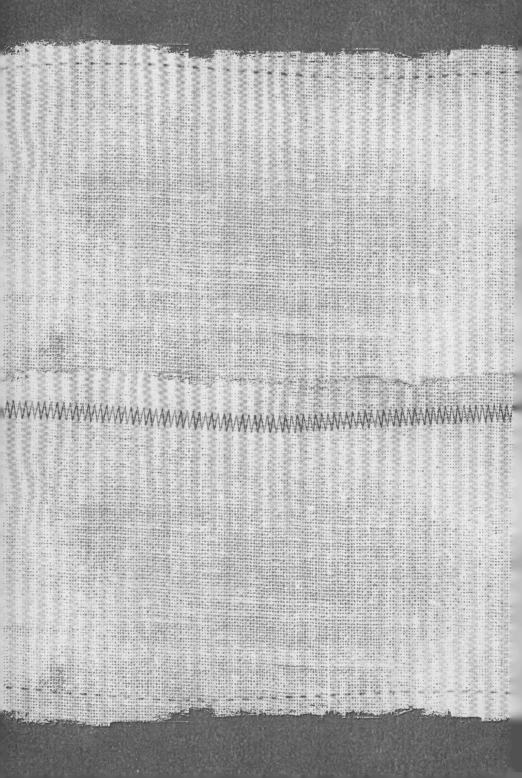

CHAPTER 3

FAMILY BACKGROUND

GRANDMOTHER'S FAMILY • Nonna's mother's family, the only extended family Nonna knew, was very important to her; she cherished their memories until her death. At the end of her diary transcription, she included more background information on Yakov and Feodosija's life and family.

Nonna's maternal great-grandfather, of whom she and her family were very proud, was a Russian count and a Cossack—a member of an autonomous people group in Asian Russia or Eastern Europe whose name means, roughly, "free person." Nonna's maternal grandfather followed in his father's Cossack tradition.

Nonna never met this charismatic grandfather, but as a child she looked at his portrait above the fireplace mantel at Grandmother's house with great love and admiration and loved to hear her grandmother's many stories about his good looks and courage. Nonna wrote, "My Grandmother, Feodosija Nikolayevna Ljaschova (born the daughter of Count Nikolai Andrevejevich Kozlova and Countess Maria Fedorovna Kozlova).

Beyond this point, the true names escape my memory, if I was ever told. There are no written documents about them in my possession." It is likely that the *Andreyevich* spelling was intended instead.

Nonna also mentioned her grandmother's grandmother, who lived to the age of 114 years, and who, according to Nonna's grandmother's stories, climbed up on a roof at age 114, fell off, broke her hip in two places, and died from infection and gangrene.

Novorossisk, Russia, 1917

My great-grandfather's name was Alexander Alexyevich Ljaschov. He was a count and also a Cossack. He fought in the war with the Tatars around Odesa near the Azov Sea. He was killed in the war somewhere near Odesa. His son, Yakov Alexandrovich Ljaschov, was to become my grandfather.

YAKOV ALEXANDROVICH LJASCHOV • Nonna's transcript gives her grandfather's name as both *Jacob Alexandrovich Ljaschov* and *Yakov Sergeyevich Ljaschov*. Because Yakov's father's first name was Alexander, Yakov's second name was most likely Alexandrovich, so we have used that name. It is possible that the *Sergeyevich* Nonna mentions belonged rather to Yakov's father, whose name she gives as Alexander Alexyevich Ljaschov.

I never knew my grandfather but was told many stories about him and his life when I was growing up as a child. My grandmother had an oil portrait of Grandfather, and she would hang it above the mantel over the large fireplace in the Great House when the family was all together. When the family left, she would take the portrait down, carefully wrapping it in blankets, and would store it in the attic due to the political changes that had taken place during the Bolshevik Revolution.

Grandmother would gather all her family around the fireplace in the evenings and tell the stories about Grandfather and his life, and about what a loving, kind man he had been. My, he looked dashing and courageous wearing his white Cossack uniform, with his sword hanging down by his side.

GRANDFATHER'S PORTRAIT • Grandmother hid the portrait of Grandfather, who had served the last Tsar, because at the time of Bolshevik rule, Nicholas II sympathizers were in grave danger. Feodosija wanted her children and grandchildren to know the family's past, but she instructed them to keep it secret.

My grandfather married the daughter of a wealthy landowner whose name was Nikolai Dezhnev, and her name was Feodosija Nikolayevna Ljaschova. From this marriage, six children were born: Ivan, Xenja, Anna (my mother), Leonid, Antonja, and Zhenya. My grandfather was a wealthy landowner, and he owned seven grain mills scattered in southern Russia and the Ukraine. His land holdings were huge, and at each grain mill there was a dacha with a hired hand to take care of it when my grandparents were away at the other mill sites. I know that the favorite place of all was in Konstantinowka, where they had a thirty-seven-room house referred to as the Great House.

My grandfather grew up steeped in the Cossack traditions, and it was natural for him to follow in the footsteps of his father and become a Cossack. He was accepted into the Imperial Cossack Army in 1907, and in 1909, he was named to a post in the Imperial Guard Staff and was honored by Tsar Nicholas II as a faithful servant to the Tsar. In 1916, Grandfather assumed a post in the Imperial Protection Unit to protect the Tsar and his family during those troubled times when the Bolsheviks were preparing for the Revolution. The beginning of World War I was imminent, along with the internal struggles that were going on inside Russia. My grandfather was engaged in transporting people of influence out of Russia, where the center of the revolution was taking place. The revolution reached its peak in the fall of 1917, and everything in Russia was in chaos. It was late fall, and my grandfather and grandmother had made plans to leave their home and to flee from Russia and attempt to sail from the Black Sea to Romania or some other safe place.

Feodosija Nikolayevna Ljaschova (my grandmother), along with her six children were waiting impatiently and with much anxiety for her husband and their father, Yakov, to return. The trunks were packed with as many belongings as they could risk taking along. It was all planned carefully that as soon as Yakov returned, they would take a long journey—perhaps across the sea into a safer location. Yakov was about two hundred kilometers from home with just one more train (perhaps the last one) with the few lucky ones that would make it. Yakov could not abandon these people—after all he was a Cossack and was proud to serve his country—Mother Rossija—and His Majesty Tsar Nicholas II. He was a man of strength and courage, and it would not be long now that they would cross the most dangerous zone, and he would fulfill his duties and return to his own family. However—the last train did not make it, and it was there in the darkness of the woods that the Bolsheviks were waiting. They had the power now, and the "dogs" had to die, since anyone that was not one of them was surely a threat to the "New Society" and had to be destroyed.

Feodosija Nikolayevna and her children were waiting, but Yakov was not coming. It was near dawn when Dimitry Ivanovich (Yakov's friend) arrived with Yakov's jacket covered with blood. He also had his pocket watch, which was crushed.

You could see the hands stopped at two o'clock—which could have been afternoon or morning; no one knew for sure. Feodosija was stricken with grief, but she had to remain strong and could not panic—now she had to think fast—the Bolsheviks would surely come to get her and the children. Dimitry Ivanovich was strongly encouraging her to take the children and flee—but the decision had to be made quickly, and they had to leave as soon as possible.

FALL 1917 • War, hunger, and angst caused Old Mother Russia to toss and turn in chaos in 1917. Nicholas II, the last Romanov Tsar, was a weak ruler. After three hundred years of Romanov rule, the Tsar's foundation crumbled. Hunger, poverty, and the Bolsheviks proved stronger than Nicholas's imperial government. His empire finally collapsed at the hands of the Bolsheviks. The Tsar abdicated, putting his friends and followers at great risk.

Feodosija, the maternal grandmother Nonna loved so much, waited in vain with her six young children for her husband to return and take them to safety. Feodosija was a strong, courageous woman and an active member of the Russian Orthodox Church. She made sure each of her children, and later her grandchildren, were christened as infants by a priest in the Russian Orthodox Church.

Yakov and Feodosija owned several villas that were scattered across the south. There were dachas and windmills (or water mills) along with some fine houses. However, there was one place in the Ukraine, an area untouched by the troubled times, and it was close enough to Poland and the rest of Europe to perhaps provide an escape route. The name of the place was Konstantinowka (Santurinowka), where Yakov owned a mill along with a fine house; it was a large house where they had spent many summers. The Ukrainian people there were not involved in the changes that were taking place in the rest of the country. There was a big orchard at the estate—large enough to grow fruit for a profit. The friend who had brought the sad news about Grandfather was willing to help Grandmother make a quick move.

Feodosija was a woman of courage, and she had to save her children. She decided that no one should know about her husband and how he lost his life. Now it was a matter of survival for her and the rest of the family.

There were four horses and a carriage still in the stables, and this was good news. Now they could travel through the woods and use the narrow roads, since they had 250 kilometers to travel. God must have been watching over them, as they made the trip safely.

When they arrived, the place was still locked up and was quiet and undisturbed. It was good to find it just the way they had left it the last summer they had spent in it. It was a big and comfortable home with lots of furnishings, and the curtains were still in place. The keeper of the estate, Petrovich, had kept the gardens and the yard in good shape.

He cried when he was told of the sad news about his "Master Yakov." He had a great respect for him and never wanted to leave and go anywhere else. Yakov and Petrovich used to talk about "Mother Russia" and her oncoming downfall, and they shared good feelings about the Tsar. There was no news about the turnover and the chaos that was happening in the rest of the country. The people in this small part of the Ukraine were too busy with their lives and paid little attention to the big changes that were taking place all around them.

"ONCOMING DOWNFALL" • On July 17, 1918, the Bolsheviks murdered Tsar Nicholas II, his wife, and their children. They had earlier sent them by train to Siberia—to Ekaterinburg—and forced them to live in a house on Liebknecht ulitsa. Revolutionaries shot the family and speared them with bayonets. Then they cut up their bodies, soaked them with gasoline, and burned them in a bonfire. Thus ended three hundred years of Romanov rule in Russia.

No doubt the deaths of the Tsar and his family upset Feodosija deeply. She and her husband, the Tsar's loyal Cossack, had loved and respected Nicholas II and his family. It is likely that Feodosija's life, as well as her children's lives, were in danger from the Bolsheviks too. Nonna described her grandmother as "a special person," "full of love and caring," who made a tremendous impact on her life. "She, too, had many heartbreaks in her own life, but she never complained, and told us mostly happy stories."

Petrovich had been with the Ljaschov family for many, many years. He stayed in Konstantinowka, taking care of the Great House and its orchard, the horses, and a dog and a cat. The cat's name was Katja, and she lived her full "nine lives" to become an old cat. Petrovich was the caretaker of the estate while the family was living in other parts of southern Russia, where Grandfather would tend to his other grain mills. Grandfather was dependent on Petrovich to take care of the Great House, where the family would come to spend some time during the summer months. Sometimes they would arrive with a new baby that had been born in one of the other places where Grandfather owned grain mills—like my mama, who was born in another town—Novorossisk. Then others like Aunt Tonja or Uncle Zhenya—almost all of my aunts and uncles were born in different places. I really don't remember which ones were born in the Great House—perhaps Uncle Ivan and Aunt Xenja.

Petrovich did not have a family of his own, and he lived in a cottage that was located between the orchard and the stables. He was alone, and I don't know where Grandfather found him or how he became such a trusted and beloved employee of the family. However, he was a kind man, and we all liked him very much, especially the children. We loved to visit him in his cottage because it was so cozy there. Petrovich would tell us some funny stories and play games with us such as checkers, cards, or even chess. When we came to visit Grandmother, we all looked for Petrovich as soon as we arrived.

Petrovich had been working for my grandfather and grandmother for so long that he was just like a member of our family. Many of my fond memories as a child revolve around him and the time he shared with us.

PETROVICH • Nonna carried a photograph of Petrovich in her pillow during the Holocaust. She greatly loved and admired the caretaker of the Great House. It seemed that Petrovich became a sort of surrogate father and protector for Feodosija's children after the Bolsheviks killed Yakov. Nonna described Petrovich as a "trusted and beloved employee of the family," a "kind man . . . we all liked him very much—especially the children."

CHAPTER 4

MAMA'S FAMILY

Yakov Ljaschov, my grandfather, married Feodosija Nikolayevna. They had eight children, two of whom died as babies. The surviving children that I knew and remember were Ivan, Xenja, Anna, Antonja, Leonid, and Zhenya.

Uncle Vanya (Ivan) married Olga Pavlova, and they had five children:

Dimitry
Halina
Aljoscha
Later two more children were born—their names escape
   my memory.

Uncle Vanya and his family moved to Taganrog, the place we used to live and where I was born, into our old home, and it was there that he lived with his wife and children until his death. He was a test pilot, and his plane exploded over the Azov Sea in the late 1930s (just before World War II). His wife, Olga, and the children remained in Taganrog until the Germans moved in.

Aunt Xenja married Vladimir Stepanovich, whose family were owners of many coal mines in and around Uralsk prior to the Revolution. They had no children. Aunt Xenja spoiled me in every way possible. She would have me over at her always luxurious and expensive apartments after they moved to Konstantinowka. She would tell everyone that I was her daughter. Uncle Vladimir would go along with her stories—and he looked like a "papa" too. Mama, however, did not approve of Aunt Xenja's spoiling me and letting me do things without her approval. However, Aunt Xenja was my favorite aunt, and I loved her and all her sophistication.

Anna, my mother, met Yevgeny Lisowsky in St. Petersburg (Lenigrad) while at the university studying art and music. She was still very young at that time; Yevgeny was nine years older. He had already gotten his degree and was working on his master's degree in languages and studying the history of Europe. Papa was originally from Warsaw, Poland, and came from a very wealthy family called *Lisowsky* (or *Lisowitz*). His grandfather owned at least seventeen estates all around Warsaw and southern Poland and in the Ukraine. His dad's (my grandfather's) name was Johan Lisowsky (as far as I was taught). There is a strong possibility that my father changed his name from *Lisowitz* or *Lishkowic* to *Lisowsky* to give it a Russian sound. This is speculation on my part, because my father called himself Yevgeny

Ivanovich and it was common for all Russians to take on a second name from the first name of their father. For instance, my name is Nonna Yevgenyevna Lisowskaja (the ending *aja* means a female name and the ending *y* or *i* means a male name). Or like my mother's name: Anna Yakovlevna *Ljaschova*, unlike my uncles' and my grandfather's name, which was *Ljaschov* (no *a* on the end).

SPECULATION • Nonna suspected her father came from a Jewish family in Warsaw, Poland. But Yevgeny never confirmed the fact with Nonna. She never met her father's family.

Aunt Tonja was my mama's youngest sister; she was petite and beautiful with almost-blond hair. Like my grandmother, she was a homemaker, and her life revolved around her home and her children. She married a chemical engineer whose name was Alexey Vassiliev. Unfortunately, she lost a few children through miscarriages and one little boy to a dysentery illness when he was only two years old. Her surviving children were both girls.

> Ljonya (died in childhood)
> Zina
> Luci

Uncle Ljonya (Leonid or Leon) was in his late twenties the last time I saw him. He was a very gentle and shy young man with great intelligence and character. He remained a bachelor and was deeply involved with chemistry, physics, and science in general. He rarely stayed at the village home, and Grandmother was forever concerned about Leonid not having a family of his own or being settled down.

And there was the youngest Ljaschov—Uncle Zhenya—

who was Grandmother's pride and joy. He not only inherited all the good looks from his father, Yakov, but Grandmother had a great dream of seeing a handsome Cossack in him—following in his father's footsteps. It broke Grandmother's heart when he decided to join the air force in Irkutsk, and when she saw him in that dark blue uniform (in spite of his incredibly handsome appearance), she shed many tears. It was not the uniform of a Cossack, and that was a dream that had not come to reality for Grandmother. However, her disappointment intensified even more when Zhenya decided to marry a girl from a family of a "common" background. Even in those troubled times, Grandmother could not "see" one of her children marry someone with a different background. But Zhenya's love for that girl overpowered the love for his mother's heritage and wishes.

His wife's name was Nadezhda (Nadja), and she was really quite beautiful and smart. With only a high school education, she made a good wife and later a caring mother for Uncle Zhenya's baby—and maybe more children. I never saw them after that one visit they made (Zhenya, Nadja, and the baby) to the house in Konstantinowka (Santurinowka) in 1937 or 1938. They lived in a far place named Irkutsk, in Southern Siberia, where Uncle Zhenya served in the air force.

GRANDMOTHER'S PREJUDICE • Nonna never explained what Grandmother meant by "common" or from a "different background." Feodosija became upset when her youngest son, Zhenya, married a "common" girl. Possibly, Nadja's family had no wealth. This glimpse into Feodosija's feelings suggests that she had objections to the spouse of another child of hers, Anna: there is suggestion that Yevgeny was from a Jewish background.

CHAPTER 5
Educating Anna

Feodosija knew that she had to find some way to educate her children. Anna was a talented one, and at the age of seven, she was already showing interest in painting, music, dancing, and being artistic in general. Yes, Anna (perhaps she was one of Yakov's favorites) should be taught music. Yakov had great plans for her education even when she was a small girl. Feodosija had to find a place where they could all be taught proper manners and get an education.

The friend who had helped them move offered to help place Anna in a conservatory in St. Petersburg, since he had some friends of influence there and he could arrange for her transportation. Feodosija agreed without hesitation since Anna had beauty and talent and she was aggressive enough to be away from her mother. Music and art had to be taught at an early age, and St. Petersburg was the place that most Europeans sent their offspring to study. It was a place of great opportunities in spite of all the turmoil surrounding it. There were also many young people that were participating in the revolutionary movement, but no one was really concentrating on politics there. Most people were too involved in more sophisticated ideas like art, music, ballet, etc. This would be a good place for Yakov's daughter, Anna. The decision was made to send her there.

Anna was doing beautifully in her studies and was also growing up to be a beautiful young lady—probably faster than her family realized. While at the conservatory, she met a student from Warsaw, Poland, who had an influential background. He was nine years older than Anna. His name was Yevgeny, and his family was one of the wealthiest in Warsaw. He had spent many years at St. Petersburg studying.

They fell in love, and they traveled to Ukraine to meet Anna's mother. If Anna could marry Yevgeny, her family would have a great opportunity to get out of Russia. After all, with the kind of influence that his family had, there could be all kinds of opportunities for them to get out. Transportation out of troubled Russia could still be bought with gold, jewels, and money.

However, Anna was not old enough to get married, especially since the Orthodox Church was still very active, and no Orthodox priest would perform the ceremony. But even in this situation, a small donation of gold would get the job done.

Arrangements were made for Anna's wedding, and Feodosija signed a consent agreement. The small but beautiful wedding was attended by only family and close friends and was held in the Orthodox church near the villa at Konstantinowka, with the priest conducting the ceremony. He was paid a sizable sum in gold for the favor and the work that he did.

THE ORTHODOX CHURCH • A woman who married outside the Russian Orthodox Church was not considered a legal wife but rather a man's mistress. The church also had strict rules about underage women getting married, and Anna was under the minimum age requirement. Her mother, Feodosija, gave her written consent in order for Anna to marry at such a young age, in the summer of 1923, and paid the priest a large amount of money.

Anna and Yevgeny became man and wife, but Yevgeny had to return to St. Petersburg, leaving Anna with her family for a while. He had some plans worked out that included his first attempt to move Anna and her family out of Russia and to Poland. His plans failed, and he soon returned without success and started to work on another plan. However, things were moving too fast, and the Bolsheviks were putting a strong hold on the exits out of Russia. After several attempts to get out of Russia and back to Poland and his family had failed, Yevgeny tried to find some kind of way to remain in Russia and to protect Anna and her family from the danger of being "found out."

For a while, Yevgeny was able to get some money and some gold from his family. This helped keep his hopes up. Also, during the Depression gold was the best source for survival. However, as time went on and the Communists took a strong hold on everything—they would put anyone in chains who didn't cooperate or who would look unfavorably toward them—Yevgeny and Anna started to make a kind of life for themselves; and her mother, Feodosija, became more dependent on their help.

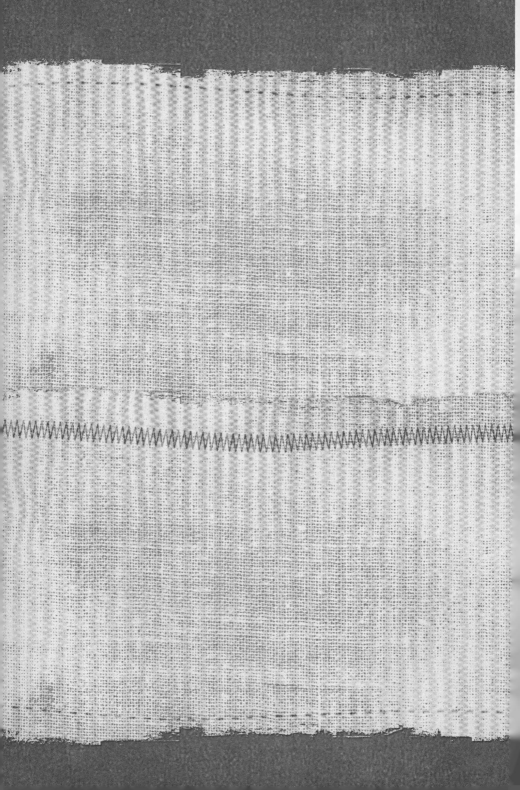

CHAPTER 6

MOVE TO TAGANROG

After Papa had failed to find a way out of Russia, he and Mama decided that they would have to start a life of their own. In the winter of 1924, they moved to the city of Taganrog—a city that was located on the Azov Sea. Grandmother owned a house there that was vacant, so Mama and Papa moved into Grandmother's house. All the furniture and furnishings had been left in the house, so the only things they had to move were their personal belongings.

They traveled from Santurinowka to Taganrog by train, and what a beautiful train ride it was—the scenery in that part of the world is unique and so beautiful. Papa had wanted to move to Taganrog because this was a city of international trade with the ships from Europe and other parts of the world, coming in through the Azov Sea. This would give Papa exposure to the people from Europe and would possibly open an avenue to get out of Russia.

The house they moved into was a beautiful two-story home with a view of the waters of the Azov from the second-floor windows. There was also a cool, soft breeze blowing at all times. The house had two wrought-iron balconies that would allow one to enjoy the view of the sea and also the cool breezes from the water.

Mama and Papa were so much in love. They were both very happy in their new home. Papa worked as an interpreter at the port and also had time for his hobbies—photography and woodworking. He spoke six languages fluently and had a working knowledge of three more foreign languages, so his skills were always in demand whenever foreigners were around. The house was located on a street that was named after the Russian poet, Chekhov—it was called Chekhov Lane or Boulevard—because here is where Anton Chekhov was born and lived for many years.

TAGANROG • This town, in the Rostov oblast, or province, is situated on the Sea of Azov, near the River Don. Nonna was born there in 1927; it is also the birthplace of Anton Chekhov, in 1860.

Yevgeny and Anna had traveled there from Santurinowka, also called Konstantinowka, having been annexed to the latter at some point in time. This explains why Nonna uses the two towns' names, or a combination of them, interchangeably.

On November 3, 1925, Anatoly (my brother) was born, and Mama and Papa were very happy about getting their family started.

Two years later, on September 22, 1927, I was born. Papa

gave me the name Nonna, which originated from the Greek name *Nonnatus* and had been used in his family for a very long time.

NONNA'S BIRTH • Papa named Nonna after St. Raymond Nonnatus—*non natus*, meaning "not born"—the patron saint of mothers and midwives. His mother had died giving birth by caesarean section.

They say that memories do not go beyond the age of two years or so, but that is not so. I remember so well the times that we lived in that house in Taganrog—the lacy curtains on the long windows in the bedroom where my cradle was placed. It was very close to the window. I remember Mama singing a lullaby to me while she rocked the cradle. Actually, it was a small bed that was fastened to rockers. I remember Anatoly's small bedroom, full of toys and books. That bedroom had only one window, and outside that window there was a tree. I remember dropping my china doll and crying very hard as I looked at the broken pieces scattered on the floor.

We were fortunate enough to have a *nanja* (nanny) to look after Anatoly and me. I can remember that she had long black hair and that she looked very tall to me. I really didn't like her because she would try to coax me to eat Cream of Wheat, which I didn't want. I would turn my head away as she was trying to force a spoonful into my mouth, and I would spit the Cream of Wheat out. This would make the nanny very mad, and she would try even harder to force me to eat.

"CREAM OF WHEAT" • Developed in 1893 at a mill in North Dakota, Cream of Wheat might have been on young Nonna's table. But it is also possible that in transcribing her diaries as an older woman and a naturalized American citizen, Nonna could have used an American brand name to describe a similar local product.

Mama had a Singer sewing machine that you would pedal when you sewed, and this machine held a fascination for me. I would sneak over to the machine every time I would get a chance and pedal the thing with my small hands.

There was a birthday party for Anatoly, and the parlor (living room) was filled with children. They were laughing and running around the table where there was a big cake with three candles on it. Anatoly was fussing with a large toy that looked like a train. I also remember our rocking horse—it was covered with brown fur (or horsehide), and it stood just a few feet away from Mama's grand piano. These memories are so vivid to me that it seems that these things happened only a short time ago.

A COMFORTABLE LIFE • Nonna mentions her mother's grand piano, Anatoly's birthday party with cake and toys, and the hired nanny—as well as silver skates (later) and a music teacher. She wrote in her childhood diary: "I like my music teacher, Mlle. Jarowski. However, she is strict. She makes me stay at the piano (sometimes two hours) until I play *Tales of Hoffmann* perfectly. I'd rather skip this one and play #6 from the book, 'Barcarolla.'"

These, along with Anna's freedom to pursue creative outlets, were luxuries under the Stalinist system.

Papa was busy with his work and hobbies, but he also had many people visiting him (quite a few foreigners). He would take them into the library, where there were shelves against two walls; the shelves were loaded with books all the way to the tall ceiling. Papa would sit and talk to these visitors in a quiet voice—no one knew what they were talking about.

PAPA'S VISITORS • Foreign visitors serve as another indication of the good position Yevgeny held. Nonna remembered one "friend" in particular and wrote this about him in her childhood diary: "Papa's friend came today. I really like him. He tells funny stories in German and Polish. He makes me laugh by making 'frog' faces. I like to play chess with him. I always win. Maybe he lets me win? I think he does!"

In the corner of the library, there was a small room, latched at all times by a small hook. It was a small darkroom where Papa spent a lot of time developing negatives. The room had a small, red light that provided light for Papa to see. This room was "off limits" for my brother and me, but being curious, I opened the door one day while Papa was working. He became angry, and called for Mama to "come get this child." I saw a negative, which was on glass. When I reached to touch it, I cut my finger and got some of the fluid into the cut. I started to cry because it hurt and also because I was bleeding. I never opened that door again.

Mama was busy with her music and art, and she was quite active in the theater. Mama and Papa went out a lot at night, leaving Anatoly and me with the nanny. I have often wondered where they would go—to the theater perhaps. Times were hard and things continued to change as the world slipped into the Great Depression. However, my family was comfortable and so full of closeness and love, and I was at a young age where everything was so new and exciting to me. I knew that I was happy.

NONNA'S MEMORIES • Throughout the war years, tucked into the secret pocket of the black-and-white-striped ticking pillow, Nonna saved photographs of her mother, Anna. Some showed a newly married Anna performing on the local theater stage, dressed in elaborate costumes. The smile on Anna's face revealed her love for acting, singing, dancing, and theater.

Papa also "got into the act." Some of Nonna's treasured photographs showed Papa clowning in funny wigs and silly costumes and brought out a joyful, playful side of Papa. Despite Russia's turmoil, Anna, Nonna, Papa, and Anatoly were able to deeply enjoy life and each other in those early years together.

CHAPTER 7

MOVE TO ROSTOV-ON-DON

Amid governmental turmoil, neighbors disappearing for no known reason, and the pain and suffering of friends and family, Nonna's world began to change drastically over the next few years.

Three years before her birth, on January 21, 1924, Vladimir Ilyich Lenin died. Joseph Stalin, the "Man of Steel," succeeded Lenin as leader of Russia, eventually expelling rival Leon Trotsky from Russia. Stalin began a brutal and murderous regime, ruling Russia with an iron fist by eliminating and executing his enemies, enforcing harsh new laws, and bringing cruel hardships on his people.

By contrast, Nonna's family seems to have been spared much of their fellow countrymen's suffering—including persecution of former Ukrainian elites, such as Nonna's grandfather, a Cossack guard, had been.

It must have been in early fall of 1929 when Papa accepted a job as an interpreter with the largest and newest machinery factory in the city of Rostov-on-Don. We were moving into a very large apartment near the factory, and the factory was furnishing the apartment at no cost to us. I suppose that it was a part of his compensation package. The apartment was located near the housing that was provided for foreign visitors and was very close to the large park called Rostov's Theatrical Park. That is the place in Rostov that has stayed in my memories so vividly throughout my lifetime—it was a park in which Mama and I spent a lot of time together. I remember so well when we moved from Taganrog to Rostov-on-Don—I guess that I was two or two and a half years old. We rode the train from Taganrog to Rostov-on-Don, and after getting off the train, we rode on a streetcar to the place in which we would live for the next few years.

It was a large apartment complex with three buildings positioned so that it would look like a circle of houses with a large yard inside the circle. There in the yard were many flower beds with a fountain in the middle. On the opposite side of the apartment buildings (to complete the circle), was another large building, which was a police station (militia station). I am sure that it was a police station because there were many uniformed policemen at all times, and they had a fenced-in area with police dogs inside. Around the apartments, there was a tall wooden fence with three large gates (one between each of the buildings), and I remember that many times they would open those gates to let trucks drive up to our section and dump coal and wood down the chute under our kitchen window—it was the way down to the cellar. Each apartment dweller or family had their own cellar, and their section was a two-story one (something like America's townhouses). Our apartment was on the end of the building, and therefore it was the largest one.

We also had a private balcony—the rest of the apartments were smaller, and two families had to share the balconies and patios. I guess this was because Papa had a good job at the factory and many foreigners visited us regularly. On the back of our section, there was a hall-walkway (past the stairs to the basement, which led to the back door and out into the small backyard). It was fenced in and looked like a small garden with some trees and flowers. The upstairs bedrooms and the downstairs living room faced the backyard, and the bathroom, kitchen, and foyer faced the front entrance. We children spent most of our time playing in the backyard, but occasionally we would play with the rest of the children in the main square of the apartments.

There was also a small room with a large window; Mama called it her art pavilion. It was a place where Mama did her painting and sketching—there was an easel with brushes and oil paints, and there was always a framed canvas in the process of becoming one of Mama's paintings.

She also spent a lot of time at her piano or with her violin. There was also a bandstand, and during the Russian holidays, there was a band playing music. On the weekends (Saturday and Sunday), all the people from all the apartments were rounded up to work around the flower beds and do whatever else needed to be done to maintain the apartments. This was called "friendly labor," mainly to have something to occupy the people on Saturdays and Sundays—especially since the churches were closed down and people were discouraged from worshiping gods of any religion (Jews or Christian).

Most of the visitors to this extraordinary factory were from Germany, France, Spain, Sweden, and Norway—but there were some from America, England, and the rest of the European countries. The Russians were proud of their new factory, which produced heavy equipment and farm machinery, and they kept it open to any visitors from the West. Because Papa spoke several languages, he was very hopeful that he could still work out plans to get his family out of Russia. We had many foreign visitors come to our apartment and visit with Mama and Papa. They went out in the evenings, and sometimes they would take us along when they attended concerts or plays, but most of the time, we stayed home with our new nanja.

Her name was Varvara (Barbara), and I didn't like her very much since she was always wanting me to sit on her lap or rocking me to sleep. I just hated the way she smelled—she used too much powder and she perspired a lot, and I never liked for her to hold me close—but who could complain? We were lucky that we could hire help, since it was against the law to hire domestic help of any kind.

CHAPTER 8

A Day in the Park

In 1932, when Nonna was five years old, she wrote "A Day in the Park" with her mother. While she wrote most of her transcripts in the past tense, she translates this experience in the present tense. Since Nonna learned to read and write at a young age, and her father began her language studies early, it is possible that she wrote this event in her diary soon after the event. This snapshot of their life also showed the close relationship between mother and daughter.

Mama and I are walking and walking—but I skip at times. I am happy—so happy. It is 10:00 or 10:30 a.m., and it is springtime. The sun is bright and its warmth feels so good on my face and shoulders! Mama is humming a song quietly—something she does all the time. We are almost there. The park can be seen from the short distance. There are not many people on the streets this morning, but the nearly empty streetcars pass us by. Finally, I see the huge gates leading into the park. We walk through the gates on the wide sidewalk, and there are flowers (so bright with colors), and it smells wonderful!

My little feet are tired, and I ask Mama if we could sit for a while on one of the park benches, and Mama agrees because she is tired too. We sit on a bench, while on the ground there is a procession of ants moving very fast. I am so fascinated by the way they all march, carrying little bits of insects or whatever food they could find. Mama is explaining to me that the ants must be having a wedding.

"See these two larger ones at the front of the procession? They must be the bride and groom," Mama says.

We sit there watching the ants, and it feels good to rest our feet. Then we start to walk again and are soon in the middle of the park. There are some children with their mothers, swinging on the swings. I want to swing, and Mama thinks it is a good idea so we swing for a while.

Soon Mama is ready to read her book, and I can do almost anything that I wish as long as I am in her eyesight. I pick some flowers—looking around for fear that I am doing something wrong. There stands my favorite bush that has leaves that I like to play with—you pull one off the bush and pull off the petals one by one saying, "He loves me—he loves me not." There is a beautiful butterfly—so colorful. I want to touch it, but I don't want to hurt it. Slowly I move closer and carefully put my fingers on its wings. I can feel the butterfly struggling to get away. It makes me feel sad. Quickly I release it, and I am glad to see that it can still fly. Mama is involved in her book, but I know that she is aware of where I am because I know not to walk away too far. The sun is getting warmer, and I am thirsty. Now Mama is ready for a fresh drink of water too. We walk down the path until we reach the water fountain—the water is so cold, and it tastes good.

There is a stage platform nearby, and Mama helps me up the steps. We dance on the stage with Mama singing to our dance. We dance round and round, and we laugh and laugh. Mama lets go of my hand, and she gets off the stage. She pretends to be the audience and starts clapping her hands and says, "*Brava, brava!* The ballerina Nonna has performed beautifully!"

We both laugh and do not notice that there are some children nearby watching us—watching us and laughing also. We stroll around the park for another hour or so. Mama lets me put some flowers between the pages of her thick book and says, "We shall preserve them by pressing them in this book, and when winter comes and we can't come to the park, we will pretend that we are in the park at our house." It is a fine idea, I think, and it is a lot of fun to keep the pretty flowers this way. Mama says, "Pretty soon it will be time for Anatoly to come home from school."

And we head back home. It is such a wonderful day, and I am so happy!

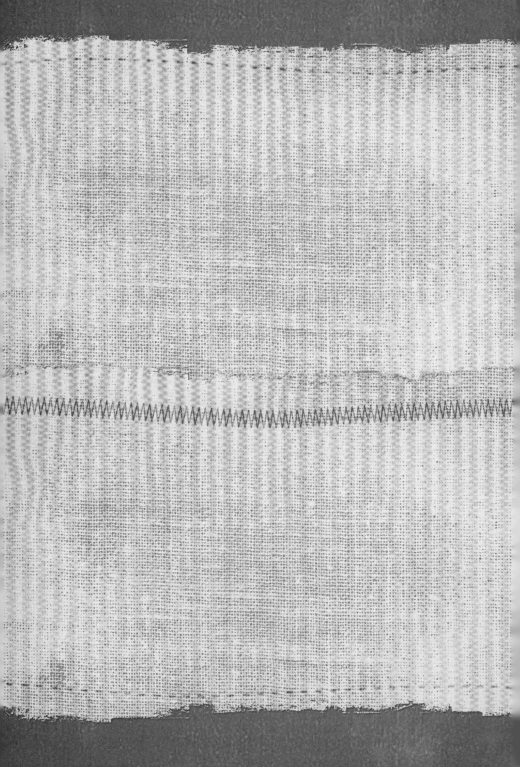

CHAPTER 9

The Depression in Russia
Stalin's Power

At this point in the thick of the Depression years, with Stalin in power, Nonna and her family began to experience some hardships. As a young child, she noticed how people around her suffered and how Russia's government placed rigid restrictions on its people. Even with wealth, food became more scarce for Nonna and her family, and they depended more on Feodosija to send food from Konstantinowka. Nonna started school in Rostov-on-Don. Nonna was smart, spoke several languages, and loved to learn. But her teachers began to question her about Papa, his family, and his background.

The Depression was in full swing by now, and people were suffering economically in Russia as they were in the rest of the world. Papa was still working at the machinery factory, and we considered ourselves to be lucky. However, food was becoming scarce, and the government had issued ration stamps to everyone. Food was being rationed, and even in our family, things like sugar and bread could not be taken for granted. I remember very well the truck with food would arrive, and people would stand in lines with their ration stamps, which they would trade for sugar, bread, flour, etc.

At the time, my grandmother was sending us packages of food from her home in the Ukraine where food was still plentiful—especially for Grandmother, since she had her own garden and was getting plenty of food from the farm people. So we didn't have it as bad as our neighbors and the other people in that large city.

The officials were still rounding up people on Saturday and Sunday to perform "friendly labor" in order to help out our "new government," which by now was beginning to take over all the businesses and factories—it was to become the "power" to all the poor. It was also a time when new rules were being issued against all religions and all believers. Most of the young people were being watched, and the children in school were being taught that there is no God. Most of the churches were closed, except for two or three of the big Orthodox churches, which remained open. But only a few of the older people attended the services. The schoolchildren were instructed to tell on their parents if they practiced religion at home. The people were watched closely, especially at Christmas and at Easter time. I remember Mama and Papa hiding our small Christmas tree in the pantry, and on Easter the colored eggs were not displayed but were kept hidden from the neighbors.

It was also a time when many people of intellect and affluence were being picked up and would never be seen again by their families. It was a time when we children were taught to be silent and not to tell—outside of our home—about our family background or anything that we knew about our families. We were instructed to never talk about anything that happened or was said in our own home. I remember so well that Mama and Papa would tell us that the "walls have ears" and that we should whisper and never talk loudly. I didn't understand what they meant. I would imagine that our walls could hear us and that there was something very strange about our home and its walls. When I would want to talk, I would look at the walls and ask Mama if I should whisper or if I could speak out.

But as I grew older, I began to understand what they meant. By the time I started to school, you could not bribe me with anything to tell about what took place at my home. There was always that feeling inside that I was somewhat different from other children, especially since I had a Polish name. After I started school, the teachers would ask me if I had any relatives in Poland, and I would just shake my head indicating no. I hated those times, because I knew that I was not telling the truth. However, to protect my family—especially my father— there was no other answer that I could give.

The name *Lisowsky* sounded as much Russian as it did Polish, and since I knew that Papa's family was in Poland, I had no choice but to deny the truth. Those were times when anyone who had families outside Russia was considered an immediate target for suspicion, and I remember that Papa told everyone that he was from Minsk, which was in *Belorusya* ("White Russia"). I believe that he kept telling people that until he died. Though we children were brought up to always tell the truth, we also understood why it was necessary to hide the fact that Papa was Polish.

HIDING THE TRUTH • In Stalin's Russia, the truth about Papa's family and place of birth might have meant a death sentence for him. Nonna was given special permission to lie in order to protect her family. Indeed, she learned early to keep dangerous family stories a secret.

This was a time when beggars were at our door constantly. They were begging for food—especially bread. I remember that the city was plagued with burglaries and robberies. Extra locks were put on all the doors and windows, and we children were instructed not to open the doors for anyone—even in our apartment where the police station was almost next door. Even with the police station so close, some of the apartments were robbed. But all through these times, Mama and Papa were happy, and they were able to provide a happy home for Anatoly and me.

Papa was doing well in his job in the machinery factory, and in 1931, he invented a machine that would slice sugar cones into sugar cubes. This created quite a bit of excitement, since people could sip their tea through this small square of sugar. Papa demonstrated his new invention at the factory's banquet, which was attended by many foreigners. He was presented an award by the German representative. We were all so proud of Papa, and we talked about this invention for a long time afterward.

CHAPTER 10

WINTER VACATION WITH BABUSHKA AT THE DACHA

CHRISTMAS

This is the kingdom of winter.

Everything is covered with snow.

The trees are whitened by hoar frost.

They seem spellbound in their new form.

'Tis a wistful but pleasant sight.

This extraordinary quiet both in the air and on the earth!

Silence everywhere!

Here I relive memories of my childhood: the thrill of leaving a warm house, all bundled up to play in the soft, new-fallen snow . . .

There are many happy events in the early years of my childhood that I like to remember. But the memories of my first trip to Grandmother's during our winter vacation will always remain precious to me. It was like a beautiful dream, except it was not a dream—it really happened, and I was there, and it was so wonderful. None of us knew what was to come!

Every year at Christmastime these special memories come back to me. This year more than any other year in the past, I have been totally consumed by the pleasant memories of the events that took place so far away and so many years ago. Perhaps it is because it all happened just a few days after Christmas as we know it today—or just before Christmas, which was celebrated by the Orthodox people according to the old calendar, on January 7.

"THIS YEAR MORE THAN ANY OTHER" • Which year Nonna is referring to is not clear; she worked on translating and transcribing her diaries for a period longer than a year.

My grandmother Feodosija Nikolayevna Ljaschova was of the Orthodox religion and a very strong believer in all that was taught by the Orthodox church. She also made sure that all of us grandchildren were taught about God properly and insisted that we were all christened as babies—naturally it was important to our grandmother for us to be christened. The pope (priest) had to do the christening!

ORTHODOX CHURCH • With Russia's churches closing all around her, Feodosija invited her family to this last Christmas at the Great House, and on Christmas Day, she took them in the sleigh—the "old fashioned way"—to the Russian Orthodox church to celebrate the birth of Christ. Not long after, Stalin closed Konstantinowka's churches, as well. Possibly because Nonna's family made sure she knew God and kept their faith vibrant and constant for her in their home, Nonna never became indoctrinated with the Communists' campaign to teach Russia's children that God didn't exist.

The Orthodox churches were still open in Grandmother's village, and even though times were changing rapidly, there were still plenty of people who were brave enough to go to church and worship God according to their beliefs. Bibles were still kept and read—and there were icons. Some of them were framed in gold or silver, some of them had a picture of the Madonna with the baby Jesus, and some were of Christ's head covered with a wreath of thorns. Most of them were painted in oil by famous artists and were very expensive—but there were also cheaper ones, which were reproductions of the real thing. Nevertheless, people stood (not knelt) before them and prayed—my grandmother had an icon in the corner of every room. It seemed that no matter from which angle you looked at an icon, the eyes of Jesus would follow you—or at least we children thought so. Grandmother would light candles in front of each icon on Saturday evening as part of the Sabbath worship.

Celebrating Christmas by the old calendar worked out very well for us for a while, because the Communist government replaced the Christmas tree with the New Year's tree, decorated by the "new believers" on New Year's Eve. St. Nicholas was replaced by *Ded Moroz* (Grandfather Frost). Of course, Ded Moroz was dressed in all white—unlike the red colors of St. Nicholas's coat. Like a good impostor of the old St. Nick, he would come with a sackful of goodies. The schools were kept open until New Year's Eve, and after school there was a big party for the children. This party was held in a large school auditorium—where there would be a huge New Year's tree erected and decorated with all kinds of beautiful ornaments. Some of these ornaments were made in the classrooms by the children themselves while being closely supervised by the teachers.

There would be music playing, and the children would hold hands and dance around the tree, which was lit with candles. The children would sing of *yolka* or *yolotchka* (the type of pine or blue spruce tree that was used). Later they would form a line "by twos" and, with great anticipation, wait for Ded Moroz to arrive. When he would appear, there would be clapping of hands and shouts of excitement. Ded Moroz would sit by the exit door with the sack full of goodies and hand out a small bag to each child. In the sack the children would find some chocolate candy, cookies, nuts, etc., and if they were lucky, they might even find a small book or a game of some sort. Then school was dismissed for a two-week winter vacation.

As for Anatoly and me, the greatest celebration and the good times were only beginning. We were packing our suitcases (stuffing them with as many things as possible) and getting ready to make the most glorious and exciting journey by train to our grandmother's *dacha*. We had the most fun-filled two weeks ahead of us, and we were absolutely ecstatic. It was going to be the best winter vacation we had ever had—especially for me, since it was my first trip to the dacha. Mama and Papa were almost as excited as Anatoly and me, but you could see the sadness in Papa's eyes because he had to stay behind in Rostov, while Mama was going with us. Two weeks was a very long time for Papa not to have us around, but he was willing to make the sacrifice just to see us having the greatest time of our lives.

CHAPTER 11

OUR JOURNEY BY TRAIN

While at the village, Babushka was preparing all the goodies and getting ready for our visit—which she called the best time of her life. We were too excited to think of anything except the train ride to Santurinowka (Konstantinowka). We rode the streetcar to one of the biggest train stations in the city of Rostov. By the time we arrived at the station, it was quite dark and very cold outside—it must have been one of the coldest winters. The days were very short in the wintertime, anyway, and by 4:00 it looked as though it was late at night.

The station was packed with people, and everyone seemed to be pushing their way to the platform where the trains were arriving and departing. With each departing train, there would be the fear that there would not be another train—or at least that was what I was thinking—but Mama kept assuring me that our train was definitely coming.

Anatoly was holding my hand tightly, as though he was afraid to lose me in the crowd. Mama trusted him completely. Even though he was only two years older than me, he was much bigger and acted very grown-up. Mama and Papa both could always rely on him to protect his little sister, and I knew too that as long as he held my hand, I was quite safe.

NONNA AND ANATOLY • Nonna possessed a deep love for her brother, looking to him for comfort and security. Anatoly played games with Nonna and read books to her. He taught her how to ice-skate. Nonna described Anatoly's departure at age fifteen as the "saddest time of my life." She was "heartbroken" when Papa sent him away on another train trip, for his own safety.

She wrote, "I never lost hope that somehow he would come home, and so many times when I would hear the train whistle, I would run outside, sit on the steps, and watch the trains for a long time thinking that he would be on one of those trains—coming home. I did that for a long, long time, all the while praying to God that this would happen, like a miracle of some kind. After all, Anatoly promised that I would see him sometimes. . . . I never got over losing Anatoly, and for many years, and all through World War II, I kept hoping that my brother would find me and come back to me. . . . I think of him constantly, and there is still a flicker of hope that he is alive."

But when our train finally arrived, we became so excited by the first sound of the train whistle that we pushed our way through the crowd, and Mama had a very hard time catching up with us. After we boarded the train and got seated in our places, it seemed as though the train would not move, but once again Mama assured us there was nothing to worry about—that there were a lot of people who had to board this train and that we would be on our way in no time. Of course, she was right again, and soon we were actually moving. It was very warm on the train, and since I was all tired out, I had a hard time keeping my eyes open. But every time I dozed off, Anatoly would give me a nudge, and make me look out the window. After a while, even all his nudges did not keep me awake. What did wake me up was the screeching of the train's brakes—it was coming to a stop.

Anatoly was checking the sign on the station and reading it out loud—"K-O-N-S-T-A-N-T-I-N-O-W-K-A." This woke me up very quickly, and in no time all the excitement took over again. There were only two people getting off the train besides us—and as we stepped off the train onto the platform, I looked at Mama and saw a worried look on her face. The first thing I thought was that Anatoly had made a mistake reading the sign and we had gotten off at the wrong station—but it was very cold outside, and Mama rushed us to get inside the station. Unlike the big station that we had left in Rostov, this one was small, and there were only a few people huddled in the corners of the benches trying to stay warm. There was a large potbellied stove burning, and it felt good just to come close to it.

Just as Mama was becoming concerned about our having to walk in all that snow and cold to Grandmother's house, through the door came this little old man—or at least that's the way he looked to me. It was Petrovich, and he was not that old then. He had a big smile on his face. Needless to say, Mama was extremely happy to see him.

"Petrovich, you know Anatoly, and this is my little one, *Nonnatchka*," Mama introduced me.

"Let's hurry—the horses are getting restless, and I surely don't want them to get chilled," commanded Petrovich.

With great amazement, I looked over at the sleigh. I was

somewhat frightened by the noises the horses were making, so I let Anatoly get in first.

"Don't be afraid, Nonnatchka," Anatoly reassured me. "It's a lot of fun to ride in a sleigh."

He was talking as though he was an "old pro" at that kind of ride. And he was right. After Petrovich threw the covers over our backs and our legs, it was warm and cozy, and even the cold wind against which we were riding did not seem to bother us too much. The roads were already packed with snow, and the sleigh was moving smoothly—there was a full moon, and there was plenty of light.

We arrived at the gates of Grandmother's home much too soon. Anatoly and I were disappointed that the ride was so short—especially since I had really begun to enjoy the whole thing. Grandmother's house was not that far from the station, and it had not taken more than ten or fifteen minutes to get there. However, Mama was very glad that Petrovich had come to get us so we didn't have to make a long walk, dragging all our luggage along.

The house was lit up, with the shutters still open—there was no electricity in the village yet, but the utility poles could be seen along the roadside. Grandmother had plenty of light in every room by using oil lamps, lanterns, and all kinds of candles. Babushka was already standing by the gate, wrapped up in her shawl. As soon as she saw us, she shouted, "They are here!" It was almost like some general had given a command—the whole army of relatives came rushing out of the house.

First out was Uncle Zhenya (Yevgeny), who was only about fifteen or sixteen years old at the time and was Mama's youngest brother. He was a very good-looking young man who, according to Babushka, had inherited his good looks from his father, Yakov. He was tall and had black hair, dark brown eyes, and a very light complexion.

"He surely would make a handsome Cossack," Grandmother would proudly say.

COSSACK • Grandmother Feodosija's compliments of Zhenya reflected her unrequited hope that her son would follow in his father's footsteps. Yakov had been a member of the Tsar's Imperial Guard as well as of the independent militant group known as the Don Cossacks.

Then came Uncle Ljonya (Leonid), who was somewhat shy and not very tall, with light brown hair and blue eyes like Grandmother's—he was probably eighteen or nineteen years old. Aunt Tonja was next—she was petite and beautiful with light brown hair (almost blond) and hazel-colored eyes. She was engaged to be married that year and was in a dream world of her own. Aunt Xenja and her husband, Vladimir (Valodya), were absent that year. Then the cousins, one by one, came running out to meet their "big city" relatives: Halina—Uncle Ivan's daughter, who was the same age as Anatoly; Aljoscha (Alexey), Halina's brother, who was about a year or so younger than I; and the last one, Ludmila, who was just a baby (perhaps two years old)—she was Uncle Ivan's littlest girl.

CHAPTER 12

HOMECOMING WELCOME

Petrovich took off as soon as he could to put the horses in the stable and put the sleigh away. He was quite tired and was ready to retire to his cottage, which was located between the stable and the orchard. When everyone was reacquainted, all the excitement began to turn to yawns—after all, it was near midnight, and it had been a long day.

After putting the baby (Ludmila) in her cradle, Grandmother returned with yet another announcement to make. Her command stirred everyone up once again: "Listen, all of you!" Grandmother went on, "I would like to make a dedication to my youngest son, Zhenya, and my oldest grandson, Anatoly." Everyone looked at Grandmother with great curiosity as she went on: "The reason that this dedication is to both of them is because last year I caught both of them sneaking out of the house at the indecent hour of 4:00 a.m., carrying their precious porcelain pots to the sewage tank." At this time, laughter broke out, and Anatoly's face turned red with embarrassment. I wanted to come to his rescue, but there was no chance, so I had to watch him endure the humiliation—until even he started to laugh along with the rest of them.

ZHENYA AND ANATOLY • Though they were uncle and nephew, the two boys seem to have played together. Nonna says that Zhenya was "fifteen or sixteen" at the time, though she might have been mistaken. Anatoly, born in 1925, would have been seven.

Grandmother continued: "To think that I always wondered why their potties were so empty and clean in the mornings."

Then Grandmother commanded everyone to follow her down the corridor, and there at the end of the hallway was this small closet with a drape drawn at its entrance. With a look of great pride, Grandmother opened the drape, and there it was!— the only one of its kind in the village—a round toilet bowl with a fine, handcrafted wooden top. It was attached to the floor, with modern plumbing connected to pipes underground and all the way to the sewage tank, which was located about three hundred feet from the house.

It was not as modern as the one that we had in Rostov. Ours had a water tank above with a copper chain and a fine porcelain knob attached to the end of the chain. One pulled the chain to flush the toilet. However, this one was extraordinary. It had a big water container in the corner behind the toilet bowl with a bucket attached to it. This container had to be filled when it got empty. This was another chore for us to do—to carry water from the well near the kitchen door. We had to take turns doing that chore, as with all of us there, it did not take long for the container to get empty.

Well, after the "dedication ceremony" and the embarrassment that poor Anatoly had to go through, everyone was really happy to have such a wonderful thing in the house. Besides, we all benefited from it by not having to carry our potties out in the cold mornings. As for me, since it was my first visit to the village, it really did not make much difference, but I was glad for Anatoly and Uncle Zhenya.

The grandfather clock, which was located in the main hallway, struck twelve times. It was long past our bedtime. Halina and I were bedded in one of the upstairs bedrooms, and it was a cozy feeling for me to sink into that feather bed and be buried under the down-filled comforter, about six inches thick. There was a feeling of warmth, security, and love all around us. And of course there was also an icon in the corner of the bedroom, and Jesus' eyes were looking straight at us; we knew that He was there watching over us, too. Before I knew it, I was sound asleep. And if I had any dreams that night, they would have had to be dreams of being in Paradise.

The next morning, while Halina was still fast asleep, I heard the patter of small, bare feet across the room. It was Aljoscha making a grand tour of the house. Having an instinct (as we all did) to protect the younger members of the clan, I followed him. I was amazed by the beauty of the house, which looked even better to me in the daylight than it had the night before. Looking around, I followed Aljoscha all the way downstairs and into the kitchen and into a small room—a pantry (perhaps six by nine feet or so). There was very little light coming through the small window, which was way up high, and there was a door leading to the cellar, secured with a hook. Inside the pantry were many shelves stocked with all kinds of jars. There were also several barrels filled with flour, sugar, rice, etc.

There was a jar of Grandmother's homemade raspberry preserves (which became my favorite preserves), and nearby was a ceramic pitcher filled with heavy breakfast cream. Both of them had been left open—like a trap that was set with the purpose of catching someone! Aljoscha spotted them before I did and started whining, "I want some; I want some!" Trying to keep him quiet, I stuck my finger into the preserves, and then into the cream, and let him lick my finger. By then, my own desire took over, and once again, I stuck my finger into the preserves and then the cream. It tasted heavenly.

Just as we were enjoying our "breakfast," I looked up, and there in the corner—yes, in the pantry—was an icon. Jesus was looking straight at me, as though He was saying, "I saw that!" I knew that I had committed one of the worst "sins"—which was to get into something without someone's permission. I had to think quickly. There, near the bottom of the shelf, was a stool. Dipping my finger back into the preserves and into the cream, I stood on the stool; and barely reaching the icon, I smeared Jesus' lips with it. Now that He had some, surely He would "forgive me."

About that time, I heard Grandmother's voice. No doubt, she had been up for hours and was coming in from outside. I grabbed Aljoscha's hand and got out of the pantry just in time. When she saw us in the kitchen, she hugged us, and that made me forget about the naughty thing that I had done.

JAM ON THE ICON • Nonna told this story to her children because it was a happy remembrance. It proved to be one of their favorite stories.

The rest of the day was a very busy one for all the grown-ups. There was a lot of baking, cooking, and getting ready for the Christmas celebration. The house was filled with a magnificent aroma.

Sitting on the windowsill, I was amazed at what I saw. There was a pond near the house, and it was iced over solidly. Two boys were ice-skating on it. There was a road alongside the pond, and now and then you would see a horse or two pulling a sleigh loaded with wood or whatever. It was a kind of quietness and peacefulness that I was not accustomed to, coming from the big city of Rostov. It was quite a change. There were no streetcar noises and not many people to see.

The birch trees (so tall that you had to look way up to see the tops) were lined up all along the side of Grandmother's house, and they stood there so proudly even though they were bare and covered with snow. Grandmother was talking quite often of the time when Grandfather had planted them. There were fourteen of them when they were planted. It was a gift from Grandfather to Grandmother on her birthday, and those trees kept growing taller with each year, with only one lost, struck by lightning.

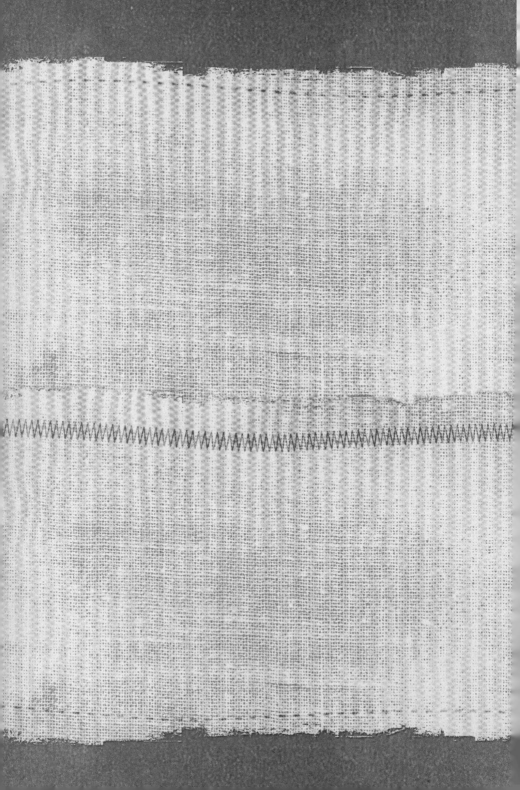

CHAPTER 13

Our Fun Time Begins

While the grown-ups were busy with the work of preparing for Christmas, we children were playing with our dolls, and the time seemed to slip by. Later in the afternoon, we had one more surprise coming—we heard Babushka calling, "Petrovich, get the horses and sleigh out! We are going for a sleigh ride!"

Grandmother herself was probably just as excited about the sleigh ride as we children were—if not more so. It was something that she had been looking forward to all year long. Petrovich enjoyed taking us for the sleigh ride more than anything else that he had to do. He had been doing this for as long as he had been with the family, and it was his favorite job in the wintertime.

While we were being dressed in our warmest clothes (caps

with earflaps, scarves, mittens, etc.), Uncle Zhenya and Anatoly were already outside opening the gates. Now I could see the bright colors of the sleigh, and I could imagine why it was called the most "famous thing" in our family for generations. It had to be touched up with oil paint when needed. It was a very large sleigh that could fit at least twelve people—and of course, the more people in the sleigh, the warmer the ride. The horses (all three of them) had bells on their harnesses, and it was very exciting.

Everyone wanted to get up front and be close to Petrovich. Once Grandmother had to enforce a "suggestion," making us take turns sitting up front with Petrovich. After we were all seated and everything was in order, we took off—what a glorious feeling! It was a very good day for a sleigh ride. The sun was out, but it was very cold (maybe 30 degrees below zero); when we breathed, we could see our breath turn into particles of ice with beautiful glitters.

The snow on the road was well packed by other sleighs, and because our sleigh was heavily loaded, there was no problem keeping the sleigh on the road. When we were far enough away that Grandmother's house could not be seen, Petrovich took a road that was close to the woods. It was Grandmother's idea so we could spot some rabbits or other animals. With the sounds of the bells and the children's noise, the furry creatures would scatter back into the woods.

"Not too close to the trees, Petrovich," Grandmother would say. "We don't want to see any wolves or wild boars." It seemed as though she really enjoyed putting a little fear into us and seeing the looks on our faces.

After the sun went down and everyone was getting hungry,

we were ready to go back to the village. Petrovich was all tired out, and after he put the horses in the stable, covering them with blankets so they would not get chilled, he was ready to retire to his cottage. But there was plenty of day left, even though it was dark outside.

The best times were yet to come. We would gather in the parlor by the *ochag* (fireplace), and Grandmother would be ready to play her favorite game, Lotto, with us. Lotto was something like Bingo, except that we pulled small barrels out of a sack, and on each barrel there were numbers, one on each side of the barrel. Someone called out the numbers, and each player would check the numbers on his or her card. Grandmother really loved to play Lotto, and the prize for the winner would be cookies or some other goodies that she had prepared before we arrived. Grandmother would end up being the biggest winner of all— then she would be sitting there with the basket full of prizes and observe the envious looks on our faces. She would finally say, "I just can't eat all this by myself! Who wants some?" Of course, we were ready to take her up on her offer, and we would fill our bellies with all the goodies—no cookies ever tasted so good as the ones that Grandmother baked.

By the time the Lotto game was over, the samovar had finished brewing fresh tea. Grandmother never let us drink strong tea—that was her treat. She would make some hot cocoa for us—cocoa was a delicacy in those days, but somehow, Grandmother always managed to have a can of it hidden someplace.

Before we got tired out and fell asleep, Grandmother would play another game with us. It was the most interesting game of all, in which she would tell us about her family's past. The rules of the game were that we had to keep these stories to ourselves and never tell anyone outside the family about things that we knew. Grandmother made us promise that we would obey her and keep the stories within us, because we loved God, our family, and our grandmother.

SECRETS • At a time in which heritage could determine one's fate, Grandmother made keeping family secrets into a game for her grandchildren. Through her many stories about Grandfather, Feodosija gave Nonna and her other grandchildren roots and a Russian heritage that they could be proud of.

Then she would point to the portrait of Grandfather, which was hanging in the parlor over the fireplace. It was the picture of Grandfather in his white Cossack uniform, with the sword hanging at his side. After we were ready to listen to her, she would tell us all about our grandfather, and how brave and wonderful he was. She would tell us about something that happened many years earlier when she was younger. Some of the stories were very sad, and she would shed some tears even while telling us the ones that had happy endings, and she would always assure us that we would see some very happy times to come. When we were bedded down, there were plenty of nice things to dream about. I now realize that this was Grandmother's way of passing on the legacy of our family, and I will forever be grateful to her for doing this.

January 6 was our Christmas Eve. Needless to say, everyone was very excited. Outside, it was snowing hard, and all of us children were scattered throughout the house most of the day. Mama and Grandmother were in the kitchen preparing for the feast. Aunt Tonja was given the job of babysitting Ludmila— after all, she was getting married soon and would need the experience. Grandmother reminded her of that quite often. Uncle

Ljonya was at the cottage playing checkers with Petrovich; Uncle Zhenya and Anatoly were in the parlor playing chess, occasionally accusing each other of cheating; and Halina and I were busy playing with our dolls and other toys. Aljoscha was everywhere in the house, or it seemed that way, since everyone was sending him to go see or bother someone else.

None of us children knew that somewhere in the stable there was a big tree (*yolka*) waiting to be decorated and that it would become "the most beautiful tree in the world!"

CHAPTER 14

CHRISTMAS CHURCH SERVICE

It was Christmas morning and all of us children were wide awake, but we were forbidden to come downstairs until Mama came for us. We were lined up (still in our nightgowns) when we heard Babushka's voice at the kitchen door. It sounded like another of Grandmother's friendly commands, and this time it was directed at Petrovich. Grandmother said, "Petrovich, I wish very much that you would dress in your holiday attire this morning—we have all our young children here, and they must have a chance to see how Christmas is celebrated. We shall travel to the church service in the old-fashioned style."

"Could I at least wear my cap instead of the top hat?" Petrovich was begging.

Soon it was settled, and Grandmother had won, as usual.

Petrovich would dress up as he had done so many Christmases before all the changes started to come about.

Mama lined us up, still in our gowns, in front of the parlor door, which was still closed. It was Grandmother who opened the door, and there, standing in the middle of the parlor, was the most beautiful, decorated Christmas tree I had ever seen. The candles on the tree were already lit, and the whole room was filled with millions of glitters and sparkles from the tree.

Suddenly everyone was wide awake, and the sparkles from children's eyes blended with the rest of the sparkles. Joining our hands, children and grown-ups, we walked around the tree at least three times. Then, starting with Grandmother, everyone started embracing and kissing, saying, "Happy Birthday, Christ." After all the good wishes were exchanged, and everyone hugged and kissed, we started to look for surprises, which were hanging from the tree. There were cone-shaped bags with our names on them, but we were instructed to leave all of them on the tree until we returned from church. This kept us children very excited, as we had something to look forward to for the rest of this wonderful Christmas day.

Fresh-fallen snow was at least knee-deep and covered everything in sight—Petrovich in his top hat and a split-tailed coat was already in his seat on the carriage and was trying to keep the horses still. There were three horses, decorated with wreaths made out of pine twigs and red ribbon tied in pretty bows—they also had bells on their harnesses—all of which was colorful, cheerful, and as exciting as the morning itself.

Everyone except Uncle Zhenya, who stayed behind to babysit Ludmila, were loaded into the carriage, which was affixed to the big sleigh itself. It was still dark outside—I don't think it was past 6:00 a.m.—and the ride to the church must have taken at least twenty-five minutes. We were all so excited. Anatoly was picking on Petrovich, and everyone was laughing because he looked so small under that hat, but we were scolded by Grandmother for making fun of Petrovich.

Long before we reached the church, the sound of multiple bells could be heard in the stillness of the early morning—we knew by the sound of the bells that we were coming closer to the church. Soon we entered a long, narrow road with tall birch trees on each side, which led us all the way to the church itself. It was a unique church: though I had been in the Orthodox churches in Rostov before, I had never seen so many onion-shaped domes and steeples in one place. Each steeple was crowned with a big copper cross—even in the dark, you could see the shine they were giving out—it looked like gold in the flicker of a dim light. One could not come close to the church and go inside without first stopping to look up and admire the array of steeples and crosses—who knows how long they had been there and how many believers had looked up and admired them. Whoever thought of the idea to build a steeple in that shape was long gone but had left something behind that would last forever.

There were five smaller steeples surrounding the big one, which was standing in the middle of them so strong and proud. The cross on the big steeple was so high that it looked like it was touching Heaven itself—it seemed that the steeples were overtaking the church building. The entrance to the church was a large door, with the top of it shaped just like the steeples.

At the sides of the door there were crippled people crowding around. (I guess they were beggars.) One man didn't have any legs, and his body was affixed to a cart, while on the opposite side there was a blind woman, and by her side was a small boy holding a cup. There were other beggars, too, around the steps that led to the big door. All this made quite an impression on us children, and I remember so well being quite frightened by what I saw.

CONTRAST • As a child, Nonna admired the magnificence of Russian Orthodox churches, the symbolism and significance of domes and crosses and steeples. But she also noticed that impoverished people stood beneath those domes begging for food and money. People were starving in late 1932, the beginning of the *Holodomor*—a Soviet genocidal starvation policy that claimed 6–8 million lives in less than one year. The poor people frightened Nonna and "made quite an impression" on her.

There were more people arriving at the same time, but they were coming in a more usual fashion than we did, especially with Petrovich being dressed like he was. Babushka was giving us children a gentle push through the large door, while Petrovich tried to keep busy with the horses. He was hoping that we would leave him behind tending to the horses and carriage—that Grandmother would not notice him—but her eye was much quicker than his cleverness. By the time he was thinking of staying out of church, Grandmother was motioning for him to come along, and Anatoly was giving him an encouraging smile. But Petrovich was only too happy to at least remove the top hat for a while when entering the church.

Inside the church, I was absolutely overwhelmed by the surroundings, the people, and the smell of so many candles—there were hundreds and hundreds of candles—very large ones and small ones. Everyone who entered the church had to take a candle and light it from one of the large candles that were on the sides of the entrance. Then each person would proceed to the center of the church. All the people re-formed in the middle of the church, where there was a table resembling a pulpit surrounded by four huge candles.

On the table, under glass, there was a huge icon in the image of Holy Mary and Baby Jesus, and one by one people would kiss the icon (the top of the glass) and place candles around it. When it came our turn to kiss the icon, Anatoly turned around. Mama gave him a look of disapproval and pushed him toward the icon. And of course, Babushka was behind us, so we did as everyone else had done, which was to kiss the icon and proceed ahead. It was so quiet as the crowd was moving on one could hear only the shuffling of feet.

Suddenly the chorus struck a loud *Alleluia*, and it seemed as though thousands of angels had filled the church. The chorus was singing the cantata; it went on for a long time, with the priest occasionally breaking into the sound of the chorus with his deep voice. The priest's attire was all in glitters, and it reflected the lights of the candles. He now and then would go behind the curtain and come out with the incense lantern, and he would swing the lantern—sending the aroma of incense everywhere.

Soon my little feet were getting tired, and I wanted so much to sit down, but there were no chairs since all the worshipers either stood or knelt. I dropped down to my knees as soon as I saw Grandmother do so, and for a short time my feet were resting. At least we children (and I am sure Petrovich, too) were really happy to hear the chorus strike the final note of *Amen*. Outside the church, people were hugging and kissing, cheek to cheek, and repeating what we had done at home, which was to say, "Happy Birthday, Christ."

As we all loaded up in our carriage, the excitement was unbearable (at least for us children). We knew that in just a little while we would be opening our cone-shaped bags and filling our bellies with the most delicious treats. The church bells continued to ring, and even the horses seemed eager to head back home to the village. Petrovich started to hum a holiday tune, and soon everyone joined in, with Anatoly standing up in the carriage and playing like he was directing a choir.

It started to snow very hard, even before we reached the village. The snowflakes were huge, and they seemed to stick to our faces. We knew that if it continued to snow for a couple of hours, we would have a glorious time ahead of us for days to come. There would be enough snow to build snowmen and igloos, and the skiing that was in order for the older ones would be great. Anatoly considered himself equal to Uncle Zhenya when the subject of skiing came up, but for Halina, Aljoscha, and me, just playing in the snow and sledding were exciting enough for us. We did not have to worry about what we would be doing for the two days still ahead of us.

The gates were open, and Petrovich let us stay in the carriage until the horses reached the back of the stable. It was obvious that Petrovich was happy to get home to get out of his "Christmas uniform." He was the first one to disappear into his cottage and change clothes; he came back in just a few minutes to put the horses away and take the carriage inside the *saraj* (sort of a garage). But before we went inside, we did not miss the chance to throw some snowballs at each other, being very careful not to hit Babushka. Anatoly grabbed a handful of snow and ran inside looking for Uncle Zhenya. Finding him, he dropped the snow behind his collar, making Uncle Zhenya chase him around the kitchen until Grandmother waved her hand, indicating that everything had to come to order at once. Anatoly had to clean up the wet puddle from the snow. But no one seemed to care about naughtiness, since there was so much excitement around us.

CHAPTER 15

CHRISTMAS DAY

1932

While we younger children were busy opening our "cones" from the Christmas tree, Grandmother and Mama were in the kitchen uncovering all the food, which had taken many days to prepare. A magnificent aroma was coming out of the kitchen, and soon the whole house was filled with the smell of vanilla, almond, ginger, and many kinds of good smells that go with a holiday feast. I really do not remember eating just three meals that day. The food was on tables everywhere, and we ate and ate. It seemed that for the next twelve days, all we did was eat! The samovar was brewing tea around the clock, and the grown-ups were doing a lot of reminiscing—except for Uncle Leonid, who was spending much of his time at the cottage with Petrovich. They were playing checkers and talking a lot about times that were now in the past. Uncle Leonid was always the quiet one. I never remember him saying much or ever being angry when he was around us—he always had a gentle look on his face, and he smiled at lot.

Uncle Zhenya was just the opposite—he was a very exciting person. His almost-black eyes would sparkle, and he had a certain wit about him. I guess he was more like Grandfather Yakov than any of the other children, and perhaps this was why Grandmother wanted him to become a Cossack, too. Uncle Zhenya and Aunt Xenja were the only ones in the family to inherit the dark brown eyes my grandfather had. The rest of my uncles and Aunt Tonja had blue or hazel eyes, like Grandmother.

Just as we had hoped, it continued to snow all day long, piling the sticky snow everywhere. The pond was covered with at least two feet of snow, and unless you knew where it was, you could not even tell a pond was there. It was the same everywhere—WHITE! Of course, there was no danger of falling into the pond, since the water had been frozen solid for a long time before it began to snow—but it was at the pond where everyone had the most fun. The snow was pushed from side to side, thus freeing the ice for skating. Uncle Zhenya and Anatoly were the experts on the ice. For Halina and me there were ice-skating lessons ahead.

First, we had to learn to skate with one ice skate made of wood—not metal. Pushing with one free foot, we went skating on the one skate. The next step was learning how to stand on two ice skates, then how to walk with the skates on snow before we were allowed to walk on the ice. It seemed so easy to walk on skates—we simply had to learn to balance ourselves. Once we learned to balance ourselves on both skates—we just had to slowly move, pushing the upper part of our bodies forward. However, there were a few falls before we really caught on—and falling on ice did hurt a little. It seemed that when we fell on ice, we landed on our tailbones—so we had somebody go along with us for a while and give us some support by holding our shoulders from the back until we were sure of ourselves. Once we took the first few steps by ourselves, we succeeded. Nothing gave us more pride and joy—we felt like a bird that has just learned to fly.

There were different kinds of skates to choose from—some had curved fronts, and we used them on hard, pressed-down snow rather than on ice. The ones with sharp points and a very thin bottom (on the sides they were kind of "blown-up") were used only on solid ice, like we had on the pond. We did not have "special shoes" then, and the skates were attached by grips that were tightened down by a skate key to the soles of any strong, high-top shoes. The wooden skates (with the wide bottoms) were used by the younger beginners and were tied with strong leather strings. The other skates were made of different kinds of metal, and the most expensive ones (which were used by the experts) were made out of sterling silver. Anatoly was given a pair of silver skates on his twelfth birthday—I shall never forget the happy look on his face when he opened the box and found those silver skates.

It always seemed that there were a lot of other children playing and skating on the pond, and there was always one bad kid who would cause a problem. There were pranks that the older kids pulled on the younger ones, and they were very naughty and dangerous pranks. Someone would say, "Take your mittens off and touch the bottom of your skate" after skating for a while; the fingers would get "glued" to the metal of the skates from the frost. Sometimes it would peel the skin right off the fingers, and it would hurt very badly. But the worst yet would be to touch the skate with your tongue—it would always cause a serious injury to the tongue, and the child would have to be taken to the doctor. Of course, we had plenty of protection from Uncle Zhenya and Uncle Leonid, and we were instructed not to listen to the other kids. When someone was caught pulling a prank on our pond, they were chased away, and never allowed to come back!

That night—Christmas Day—after all the excitement had died down, we gathered by the ochag. We heard Grandmother's stories from her life experiences, and those stories never faded away. As we listened to her, it was almost as if we were there. We were surrounded by love—and magic: the warmth from the fireplace; the smell of Christmas itself; and Babushka, sitting there with her hands folded in her lap—still wearing her beautiful dark green velvet dress trimmed with plenty of handmade lace—with her very gentle and strong voice and such a kind look in her eyes. All this remains in my memory forever. I can see her—just as she was then—anytime I want to go back to that very magical time in my life. She will always be an unforgettable image in my mind. It will never change even if I live to be a hundred years old—those kinds of memories I can keep with me and use as comfort when I feel unhappy or lonesome.

That night, after we were all so happily bedded down, the last thing that we heard were the chimes from Grandfather's clock (who knows how many chimes—perhaps twelve or less). None of us knew what Mother Nature was doing outside our windows. The big windows had shutters built from the inside, and they were shut to keep the cold from penetrating the house.

When we awakened the morning after Christmas, it was so incredibly quiet everywhere—we could hear no sounds from the outside. It was such an awesome feeling, and everyone was wondering what was happening. When the shutters were opened, there was nothing to see except the snow against the window panes all around the house. Petrovich was outside the kitchen and yelling loudly, telling us that he was working on moving the snow from the entrance. It seemed that he had dug himself out of his cottage. It was a long time before anyone knew what had happened.

All of this was very exciting for us, because we had never seen so much snow anywhere. The snowstorm had gone through our village and, with blizzardlike winds, had blown tons of snow—covering the two-story house up to the upstairs windows. Once Petrovich had uncovered the path to the door and freed the kitchen entrance, we were all allowed to dress and go help him shovel the snow away from the back of the house. No one cared how high or how much snow was up at the front of the house—we used the kitchen door for days afterward.

While we were busy shoveling snow, I saw something moving by the stable—it was a bushy red thing, and it disappeared behind the stable. Letting out a yell, I pointed in that direction; following the creature's footprints, everyone ran behind the stable, and what was there? Crouched in a corner between the fence and the stable wall was a baby red fox. It was very small—no bigger than a little puppy or a large cat. It had somehow gotten separated from the mother fox and wandered into our backyard. We all wanted to pet it and hold it, but Petrovich told us not to touch it with our bare hands, because once a human touches a wild creature, its mother would reject it, and it would surely die from hunger. So he put the baby red fox into a sack, got on a horse, and took it back into the woods. We all stood there watching him ride off, waving good-bye to our unexpected guest.

We stayed outside even after dark (which was then about 4:00 p.m.). We had so much fun, and there was so much to do with the snow, which was by now quite sticky. We built igloos with long tunnels from end to end, and we crawled through them. It was warm inside the snow tunnels, and it was then that we learned why the Eskimos lived in snow igloos and survived the cold. It really was not that cold outside, since there was no wind, and with night coming on, a full moon was out. With everything being covered with snow, you could not tell whether there was a horizon—it just seemed to blend into the sky. What was amazing was the incredible quietness—both day and night. Occasionally one could hear a dog barking someplace, and at night the howling of a wolf came from the distant wooded area.

Of course, there was plenty of noise from the voices of us children playing outside. One could smell the smoke from chimneys, which blended with the smell of frost and snow—it was a combination of smells one could never forget. It seemed that the entire time we were at Grandmother's house (twelve days), the weather remained unchanged—there was not much sun to see with, but at night the moon was always shining. After the big snowstorm on Christmas Day, no more snow was falling, but it looked as though there was enough snow to stay for months, and I am sure that it was cold enough to keep the snow there for a long time to come.

However, it was time for Mama, Anatoly, and me to head back home, and suddenly I really missed Papa and was ready to go back home to him.

These two weeks of my life made an impression on me that will last until I die. Almost every year as Christmas approaches, I can spend hours and hours remembering those glorious times. It is almost as though I am going back in time to relive it all over again, sensing all of it as it was then—the beauty, smells, love, tenderness, fun, and touches of loved ones, especially my dear Babushka. Thank God for letting me have that very special Christmas, one that will stay with me forever!

• • •

WINTER'S DAY

It was a magnificent December day,
With the frost-covered trees
Sparkling in the bright sun.
The sled runners squeaked
Over the frozen snow, as Papa
Was pulling the sled. I lay there
Staring into the bright blue sky.
What was going through my little head
At that time? I can't remember but
I was absolutely in peace,
Very happy and secure!

CHAPTER 16

REFLECTIONS ON CHILDHOOD

As an aging woman, Nonna sat up in the attic, pen in hand, remembering and recording on yellow legal pads her memories of a beautiful childhood. Here she stops the history of her childhood and just reflects on the sights and smells of those magical years when she knew such happiness, peace, and security—recollections that stand again in contrast to general accounts of suffering under Stalin at this time. Possibly in retrospect, any suffering allowed to penetrate the genuine comforts afforded by her family's wealth paled in comparison to her war experiences later.

Childhood! Why are these impressions so fresh, so vivid? I am now over fifty, nearing sixty years old, living in a foreign country far from all that is native to me, yet I clearly see them, feel them, sense their fragrance—and not only figuratively, but literally. The five senses play a primary role in the life of a child, and after sight, the sense of smell is, of course, predominant. If I want to be transported to the past, nothing makes me experience it more vividly than recalling a particular scent—for instance, the smell of French lilacs under my window at Grandmother's Great House, or perhaps that famous plum pudding that Grandmother prepared so carefully and served at Christmas time. Rum was poured over it and lit, and it was brought flaming to the table.

Somehow, memories are mostly associated with the smell of favorite foods from childhood days—such as cherry turnovers, called *pyroshki*. They were prepared and fried in the kitchen. My mother prepared them by the same recipe as my grandmother's, and the aroma would fill the whole house as they were fried. The fresh flowers—which were planted all around the house—and the blooming trees (cherry, apple, pear, peach, etc.) from Grandmother's orchard also gave out remembered scents.

I spent much of my time in the fruit orchard reading and doing my homework. Those are the times that will always strongly remain in my memories. I also read books that were more of a curiosity to me than the schoolbooks or library books. I would go through my father's library and sneak some of his books out. These books made little sense to me, at the age of eight to ten years old.

"IN THE FRUIT ORCHARD"..."THROUGH MY FATHER'S LIBRARY" • Nonna is remembering times at the Great House other than her first visit at Christmastime. Probably the memory of her father's library in conjunction with Grandmother's orchard is linked to the time when Yevgeny and Anna moved in with Feodosija, later on.

My aunt Xenja allowed me to borrow some of her books also. Her books were romances of kings, princes, princesses. I would simply devour them, and I would have many sweet daydreams. It seems funny to me now, though, because they were so innocently written. Nevertheless, I really enjoyed reading them, especially since some of them were sort of forbidden material for a young girl of my age. They seem like innocent books when you compare them with the junk that the kids today read. I would enjoy those books. They were something to be compared to the Harlequin Romances of today's times.

To me, my childhood was very exciting, as I look back over the past fifty-plus years!

CHAPTER 17

BACK TO REALITY

1933

As we boarded the train to go back to Rostov, I was excited that we would soon be back with Papa, but I felt sadness that we were leaving Babushka. Now that I am older, I realize that she had really worked hard to give her children and grandchildren a Christmastime that none of us would ever forget. Grandmother had been through so many changes, and surely she knew that more changes were on the way.

When we arrived home, Papa was so happy to see us, and of course, I had many stories to tell him about what had happened at Grandmother's house during our visit. Life settled back into a routine, with Anatoly and me going back to school and Mama and Papa busy with their schedules. Mama was very busy with her social life and was giving a lot of concerts playing the piano and the violin. Papa was still working at the machinery factory, where he had many new friends. Mama and Papa also had new friends at the University of Rostov, and we made many trips to Nachichevan where the university was located. We went by streetcar—it would take us about forty minutes for the journey from our home. Papa had some extra jobs repairing some of the university's medical and laboratory instruments, so he made many trips to the university.

BITS AND PIECES • Nonna wrote snippets about this time in an early diary. Here is one entry: "Today we spent a lot of time in the park—it was a lot of fun—just Mama and me. We will be going to the university in Rostov (Nachichevan) to see Mama's friends. Hope we can stay at Mrs. Solzhenitsyna's house for a night. It was a lot of fun the last time we were there. Why do they live next to the cathedral? I always see the Pope (priest) coming out of the side doors."

Mama had made friends with another very talented musician by the name of Mrs. Solzhenitsyna. I believe that we became acquainted with Aleksandr Solzhenitsyn during one of our visits to her home; he was with the chemistry department at the university. I always enjoyed visiting Mrs. Solzhenitsyna's home. I remember her son, Sasha Solzhenitsyn, with his funny-looking white coat, coming home for lunch. His ears were big and he never talked much, but I thought it was funny the way he would gulp down his cookies, and he would drink his milk fast. I liked the "Napoleon cake" that her cook made—it was the best!

SOLZHENITSYN FAMILY • Taissia Solzhenitsyna's husband, Isaakiy Solzhenitsyn, had been a Cossack for Tsar Nicholas II at the same time as Anna's father, Yakov, had. Isaakiy died in a hunting accident in 1918, six months before his son, Aleksandr (Sasha), was born.
   Aleksandr is known to have studied mathematics at the university, and

he would go on to live a notable life of his own, including winning the Nobel Prize for Literature in 1970.

One day, Mama and I decided to pay a visit to Mrs. Solzhenitsyna—we were especially looking forward to seeing her. It was a beautiful morning. After Anatoly had left for school and Papa had gone to work, Mama decided to keep me home from school that day to keep her company on the trip to Nachichevan. It was one of the nicest days in May, and the flowers were in full bloom. We walked the couple of blocks to the streetcar station and boarded the streetcar. There were only a few people on that particular car, so we sat by the window and looked out—watching the people on the streets rushing to work, school, or wherever.

Before we realized it, we had reached Nachichevan. We got off near the theater and walked down the street past the park and theater, close to the cathedral. Since we had no phone communications, we arrived at Mrs. Solzhenitsyna's quite unannounced, and Mama felt a little embarrassed. She did not like the idea of just "dropping in," arriving at someone's home without at least writing a note. However, this was a "spur of the moment" trip, and besides, it would have taken a few days to deliver a note. This day, Mama just felt like visiting a friend and did not feel like waiting a few extra days. It was a great idea to me! I was quite happy to skip school that one day and go with Mama. She left a note on the kitchen table for Papa though, telling him where she and I were.

Mrs. Solzhenitsyna was very happy to see us. We got there just before she was going to go shopping, so all three of us decided to go down the main street of Rostov, taking a little ride by streetcar to get there.

The first stop we made was an ice-cream parlor, where round tables with umbrellas were set up outside. We must have been the only customers at such an early hour of the day. I ate so much ice cream that I felt like my stomach was frozen. After the ice-cream treat, we headed to the bookstores. However, as we passed a toy store, Mama looked at me and said, "We really don't want to go in there, do we?" By the time she finished asking the question, I was at the entrance to the store.

I just looked at everything on the shelves, because we were always taught not to pick up the toys in the store but rather to wait until we were asked if there was anything that we wanted Mama to choose for us. My eyes caught a little plastic doll (it was a boy doll) dressed up in a sailor's uniform, with a little boat in his hand. I had that little doll for many years; it had a special place on my toy shelves. I admired that doll all the time—it was a very special toy that reminded me always of that enjoyable trip down Main Street.

On the way back to the streetcar and the ride back to Mrs. Solzhenitsyna's, we stopped in a music store, and Mama and Mrs. Solzhenitsyna bought some new music books. When we got back to her house, they tried the new music pieces and were quite happy with what they had selected. The cook had made some delicious cookies and some freshly brewed tea for us. The day passed quite quickly, and it was time for Mama and me to head back home.

As we started to leave, Mama looked up at the sky and saw ugly black clouds. The wind had picked up, and people were running to safety. Mrs. Solzhenitsyna persuaded us to stay because it was obvious that the beautiful day had taken a turn and a big storm was on the way. Mama was quite concerned about Papa and Anatoly worrying about us, but there was no way to let them know that we were safe. It turned awfully dark outside, and the priest at the church opened the big doors to let some people on the streets come inside the church.

There was no doubt that a cyclone was on the way, and we all went down into the cellar with pillows and some blankets. We spent that night (or at least half of the night) playing cards and games and singing and reading—any way that we could entertain ourselves until the storm passed over. We decided that we would have to spend the night at Mrs. Solzhenitsyna's and go back home in the morning.

This was one of those trips to Nachichevan that I could never forget. It was pleasant; yet at the same time it was exciting and scary. Needless to say, when we got home the next day, Papa and Anatoly were extremely happy to see us safe and sound.

MEMORIES OF THE SOLZHENITSYN FAMILY • Nonna's childhood descriptions of Aleksandr were accurate, and she even kept a photograph of Taissia throughout the war; it survives to this day. Despite her memories of their cook, ingredients to make a Napoleon cake, and the purchase of music, Taissia and Aleksandr lived in relative poverty in their small apartment in Rostov-on-Don. Their many family possessions and all their family wealth had been confiscated by the government. Possibly as a child Nonna never understood the state of the other family's affairs.

CHAPTER 18

TROUBLED TIMES
1933–34

Rumors of war were spreading throughout Russia, and it seemed inevitable that we were in for some troubled times. Papa was still working at the machinery factory and was in contact with many foreigners from the Western countries. We had many foreign visitors at our home, and Papa would take them into his library and have long conversations with them. I never could really understand the conversations because they were spoken in several languages. However, Papa seemed worried, even though he never talked about the situation with Anatoly and me. He spent as much time with us as he could and would always try to be cheerful—but always teaching us things that would be useful to us later on.

School was still being held, even though Russians were

preparing for war. We would have drills on what to do in the event there were bombs being dropped. The Russian Air Force would fly over and drop fake chemical bombs during these drills. The civilian population were being instructed to dig shelters in their yards. These were to be like large ditches dug in a zigzag fashion that people could jump into in case of an attack. These large ditches were covered with boards in order to keep small children from falling into them. The government was also busy installing air-raid sirens as an alarm system.

I was doing very well in school, maintaining a straight-A average. However, all these things were distracting. I remember the day I learned a lesson twice—first from my algebra teacher, Dr. Shutzburg, and then from my papa.

I didn't like my math teacher, so when he wrote a problem on the blackboard, I knew that I had to do it to him! When he asked for a volunteer to come up and solve the problem, I raised my hand up high (no one else wanted to go to the blackboard). He called my name and I marched up to the blackboard, picked up the chalk, and started to write whatever came to my mind— however stupid it was. When I got to the bottom of the blackboard, I made a "finished" sign. I really enjoyed watching the expression on Dr. Shutzburg's face as it became red with anger. He told me to go back to my desk and work the same problem exactly as I had done it on the blackboard, and I did what he asked me to do. He asked for my paper, and he wrote a big *F* on it with red pen. He added the question, "*Why?*" He then put his initials under the question and told me to bring the paper back to school the next day with Papa's signature on it.

When I got home that afternoon, Papa was in his study, and I took the paper to him and waited for what was yet to come. To my amazement, Papa started to laugh (knowing that I liked algebra and always made excellent grades). I guess he thought it was funny. But then, with a very serious look on his face, he told me that what I had done was very wrong and that my punishment would be to sit at his desk (for as long as it took) and work this same problem over again until I finished it. It took me about two hours to get finished (it was about two pages of work), and Papa looked it over and signed it and told me to take it back to school the next day. However, he told me that Dr. Shutzburg may not be as tolerant as he was. He told me to apologize and ask the teacher to give me another chance—to give me another problem equally difficult to work on.

I stood in the hallway waiting for Dr. Shutzburg; then I gave him the paper and apologized like Papa had said for me to do. I was really surprised when he said OK, and the first thing he did when he went into the classroom was to write another problem on the blackboard and call my name.

Everyone in the class had a great time watching me march to the blackboard again, and I am sure they expected to have another laugh. This time I worked very fast and wrote all the answers, step by step. I did not turn around when I had finished. Dr. Shutzburg looked it over, faced the class, and spoke in a soft voice, saying, "Now, I hope that all of you learned something from this experience and that no one will try anything funny again. And now, Miss Lisowskaja will get her grade changed from an F to an A+." From that day forward I liked him, and algebra continued to be one of my favorite subjects.

Another lesson that stands out in my memories happened when I was six years old and in the first grade. The thing I remember most was that Papa was insistent about teaching me different languages while I was very young. By the time I started school (at age five), I spoke at least three other languages really well (Polish, Yiddish, and German). Of these three languages, German and Yiddish were the easiest for me to learn, with Yiddish being the easiest—however, German and Yiddish are both similar. When I was six years old, I was very proud that I could speak different languages. One day, I got angry with one of my classmates, and I called her some names—it was very harmless—but I used the Yiddish language to call her the names. The teachers sent for Papa, and he had to come down to the principal's office and do some fast explaining on my behavior in school and why I was speaking Yiddish. Papa had to tell her that he had taught me several languages. He was very upset with me, and told me never to do such a thing again.

YIDDISH • Nonna's teachers called Papa to the principal's office because Yiddish was the language of the Jewish people. Papa had taught her Yiddish but had warned her to speak Yiddish only at home, not in public—since speaking the language of the Jews could arouse suspicions of having Jewish sympathies, if not heritage.

From then on, my every move in school was watched by the teachers. They also watched my brother, Anatoly, as well as my entire family. The teachers would question Anatoly and me and ask if we were Jewish, and from then on, I was careful to not use my language ability in school. With the rumors of war and all the suspicions from everyone, I was losing my excitement for school and was not as happy as I had been when I started school.

CHAPTER 19

CHANGING TIMES
1934–35

Most farms in the Soviet Union had become the government's "collective farms." Communists had taken over private land and livestock. During these years, Nonna's family—especially Feodosija—lost most of their wealth and property, including animals. Nonna noticed these drastic changes when she visited the Great House again.

The laws the Communist government had enforced so strictly in other villages finally became enforced in Konstantinowka, too. They greatly affected Grandmother, Petrovich, and the Great House with its mill, land, and orchards.

The next visit to my grandmother's house was in 1934–35. Things had changed quite drastically by then, and even though the Depression was easing up, the Soviet regime had taken over and a new style of life was being enforced on almost everyone. Grandmother no longer owned her horses—they had been "donated" to the collective farms, which had been organized everywhere in the villages. The orchard was still Grandmother's, along with the empty stable, but the property was heavily taxed, and almost everything owned by Grandmother had to be given away to the "new government." The house was still Grandmother's, but she was no longer considered to be a private owner, and she had to pay heavy taxes on it.

Grandmother continued to live there with some of her children, and she kept Petrovich there, too, still living in his cottage. However, he was no longer her "hired hand," since it had become unlawful to have employees. In order for him to remain, Grandmother had to make him her relative, so she called him her cousin. He continued to help Grandmother as he had done before, taking care of the orchard and whatever else that she was able to keep. Grandmother started to raise some hogs, and she had plenty of chickens, geese, and ducks, along with some goats that she kept for milk for her and her family. She gave up the mill and all the fields around it, except the land surrounding the house itself. The carriage and the sleigh remained in the stable and became precious symbols for our memories. People were told how many "living things" (goats, hogs, chickens, etc.) they could own. The rest of it had to be given away to the collective farms. The government called it "donating"—all to the cause of the new way of life for those who were "less fortunate." When the hogs were slaughtered, one could keep the meat (bacon, ham, etc.), but the skins and the intestines had to be turned over to the government. The skin was used to make leather shoes, and the intestines were used to make sausages.

The mill, along with all the property around it in the village, which had belonged to my family for so many years and which my grandfather had been so proud of, became the property of the collective farms. Grandmother denounced ownership of all of it as soon as the "new government" took over the village. The church was always there, but the doors were locked and boarded up and the worshipers stayed away. The priest had mysteriously disappeared, as well as other religious leaders—no one dared to talk about it, anyway. Grandmother put away all the icons in the attic, along with her other precious possessions. She buried some of her things in the ground in the cellar after they were packed in heavy metal trunks. None knew when a group of the new "militia" would appear and search the house, taking away whatever they wanted. The Bibles and the icons were burned right on the grounds where they were confiscated, and religion became a forbidden thing—all those who rebelled and dared to continue to practice it were arrested and sent away to Siberia.

The Great House was divided up into sections with private entrances, and some of Grandmother's children and their families were living in them. Many of Grandmother's family had began to come back home. To those of us who had lived under different circumstances, this new government was becoming intolerable, but there was nothing that we could do to fight it.

Mama and Papa were talking about moving back. In 1937, we left the city of Rostov-on-Don and moved into that house also. The village of Santurinowka was annexed to the town of Konstantinowka and became known as such. Soon after, the streets were named, and many new buildings and stores (mostly food stores) were built around our home. The streetcar tracks were extended, and the streetcars began to travel all the way past our street—about three miles past our street, they would turn around and go back to the original town of Konstantinowka.

We still had many neighbors who remembered Grand-mother as she was before it all changed, and they treated her and her family with great respect, as they had done before. It was very difficult for Grandmother to accept this new lifestyle, but she was forced to, in order to blend in with the rest of the people and survive. Although she had to make many changes, she remained just as proud and as courageous as she had always been. Her beautiful clothes and jewels were packed away—some of the gold and silver and precious stones were packed in the trunks that had been buried along with Grand-father's portrait, uniforms, watches, and other expensive memorabilia. Grandmother could still give her loving commands to her children and grandchildren, and to all of us, she was still "Babushka," whom we all loved so very much!

"HER LOVING COMMANDS" • Nonna described her grandmother as kind and loving but also as "strict" and "command giving." Feodosija had probably learned to be firm and strict, as well as courageous and enduring. As a young woman, she lost her husband through violent death and became a single parent to six children during the collapse of the Romanov dynasty and the Bolshevik Civil War. Feodosija proved herself a survivor, a strong Russian woman.

CHAPTER 20

WINE-TASTING TIME

*Even in these troubled times, there are many
happy and sweet memories that stay with
me, such as the story told in this chapter.*

Nonna included happy memories along with the more sober stories in her
transcripts. She remembered the wine-making days as good ones spent
with her family, and she wrote about them in detail.

One of my grandmother's specialties was making homemade
cherry wine. The wine tasting took place in the orchard where
there was a table set up, and the judges usually were her older
children: Uncle Ivan; Aunt Xenja and her husband, Volodya
(Vladimir); Mama; and Aunt Tonja (Antonja).

Grandmother was very proud of her wine making. Every

spring the orchard would break out in the most beautiful blossoms, meaning it was time for this special occasion to take place. She would open the wine bottles that had been stored in the cellar from the wine-making season (in the late summer) of the previous year. She had all the equipment for wine making, which consisted of special brass pots, tubing, etc. During this time, Grandmother was very busy for at least eight to ten days. She had a short window of time to get the wine made when the fruit was ripened to its peak. The children were assigned the job of picking the cherries off the trees and bringing them to Grandmother. Then she would take over.

Needless to say, we children were looking forward to the task, since we could climb the larger trees, and the temptation to fill our bellies with ripe cherries was too strong to resist. For the next few days of work, we all had upset stomachs, and Grandmother would line us up and give us castor oil. You could not find a place to hide to escape from Grandmother's treatment.

She had two kinds of cherry trees. The larger cherries were used by her to make cherry preserves, and the small cherries (dark red ones) were used to make the wine. We all enjoyed the preserve making because Grandmother would let us taste some of the top of the boiling mixture called *shum* (foam) as it came to the surface. It tasted heavenly. We children would line up for the treat, and she would fill our cups.

The empty wine bottles, which had been used the previous summer, were filled with wine, and the bottles were closed with corks that had narrow tubes inserted into them. This was done (as Grandmother explained) to allow gases to escape. You could see the bubbles coming up to the top and out of the bottles, allowing the wine to ferment without exploding the bottles.

Occasionally, a tube would become plugged, and the bottles would explode like little bombs. To prevent any damages or injuries, Grandmother would have Petrovich, her helper, bury them in the sand in the cellar.

Somehow, she would end up with enough wine to last to the next wine-making season (sometimes longer). Grandmother would serve her wine with every large meal, but she didn't let anyone drink her wine "just anytime." It was also served on special occasions such as birthdays and holidays.

There were some funny times when Grandmother would throw the remnants of the cherries used in the wine making to her flock of geese. She raised the geese to be used for the Christmas holidays and other times when meat was needed. We never baked turkeys—just chicken and fat geese. Beef was used sparingly in those times—the cattle were usually given to the government's collective farms and slaughtered for the government's meat markets. However, the people were allowed to raise hogs and poultry.

Let's get back to the funny times—feeding the geese the cherries. One morning, we heard Grandmother let out an alarming, desperate yell. She had gone in back of the stable, and she saw a whole bunch of geese rolling around on the ground and acting sick. She was desperate and called a veterinarian to check on her geese. The veterinarian told Grandmother that the birds had gotten drunk from eating the wine cherries. We all got a big laugh out of that, and we picked on Grandmother for a long time. It was quite a funny story.

Grandmother's orchard was very large, and she had many other fruit trees there: apples, peaches, pears, and plums (she made some plum wine also). But mostly cherries were used for preserves and wine making. These were just some of the happy memories from my early childhood, and these memories will be cherished forever.

After World War II started, Grandmother had to give up her wine making due to the shortage of sugar, which was needed for making wine. Everything was disappearing fast. But the trees kept blooming every spring, and there were always plenty of cherries and other fruit. Every spring, the whole area around the orchard would be filled with the heavenly smell of the blossoms. Grandmother would let everyone in the neighborhood help themselves to the fruit, since selling it was not possible—money had no value due to the war. However, sometimes Grandmother and other people would trade one thing for another (whatever they had). Everyone was helping each other to survive in any way possible.

CHAPTER 21

TIMES OF UNCERTAINTY

1937

When we moved back to live in Grandmother's Great House, along with other members of the Ljaschov family, we had everyone together again. Each family had their own living quarters in the huge thirty-seven-room house, and yet we were close to the ones that we loved. In spite of the uncertain times, there were also times that we could act as a family unit, and certainly Grandmother was the leader in pulling this all together.

Papa and Mama opened a portrait and photography studio in Konstantinowka, and Mama busily engaged herself in working in the Little Theater at the Civic Club, which was next door to the studio. She also organized a music club for young girls at the Civic Club, and spent a lot of time doing these things. Papa was also still trying to find a way out of Russia for his family, and as the certainty of war escalated, he redoubled his efforts. Papa continued to communicate with his Romanian college friend who was trying to help Papa get out of Russia—to anyplace in the West. Papa made a trip to Yalta in the Crimea (a resort area) on the Black Sea to meet with his friend. This time he was willing to go to Romania as the first step to freedom. Papa spent several days in Yalta and made some plans that his friend was to work out as quickly as possible.

"LOVE MY BROTHER" • Nonna and her brother were close. In the winter of 1935, eight-year-old Nonna writes of her love for him: "Love my brother, Anatoly. (I am 8 years and 3 months old—Anatoly is 10 years old.) He reads so well and makes funny faces—he makes me laugh a lot. He teaches me to ice-skate and ski—we spend a lot of time on the frozen pond. We play chess (and I beat him twice today)."

There were more pressing problems that Papa was faced with involving my brother, Anatoly. In those times, when young men reached Anatoly's age, the Soviets would place them into a communist youth group, a *Komsomol*, and later draft them into the army. Papa was strongly opposed to having Anatoly join the Komsomol and becoming a communist. However, the only way young men could attend the university was if they were members of the Komsomol, and this presented yet another problem for Anatoly. Plans were considered to send Anatoly away to live with some distant relatives in Riga, Latvia. However, Papa took Anatoly to St. Petersburg and enrolled him in the university, where he was to live with some relatives. I am sure that Papa utilized his connections with influential people to get Anatoly enrolled in the university.

This was a time of sadness for me since I didn't understand what was going on, but I could see the looks of concern in Papa's eyes, and I knew that we were in trouble. During these times, Mama and Papa were having emotional outbursts between them, since Mama was against sending Anatoly away. But she was trying to reassure me that everything was all right and that this was the right thing to do. For the first time in my life, I resented Papa's ideas, but there was nothing I could do about it.

THE LAST REUNION • Grandmother planned a family reunion in 1938, which was the same year Hitler annexed Austria. Every member of the family came. That event proved the final time Nonna's entire maternal family came together. Nonna remembered this reunion in great detail. She also kept photographs of this event hidden with her throughout the war. These photos have survived to this day.

In the summer of 1938, I remember a family reunion. Everyone in the family was there at Grandmother's Great House. Even those who lived away from home were there for this reunion. The cherry trees had finished blooming and were loaded with cherries—too green to pick. The other trees were loaded with fruit, which would be ripe in the next few weeks. The orchard was very shady and cool that very special night that we had our dinner in the garden. Grandmother put up two big tables and covered them with tablecloths, and the older members of the family helped Grandmother with the dinner. We children (nine of us) played with the ducks in the pond inside the backyard that Grandmother had built just for the ducks. She even had some water lilies planted there. We would sit there with our feet in the water and feed the ducks. Every one of us had little ducklings named after us.

GRANDMOTHER'S DUCKS • Nonna had a special love for these ducks. In 1935, Nonna wrote about the ducks: "It rained all night and the pond is overflowing—poor little ducks! My favorite is the one with the white tail—I call him 'Pierre.' He comes out of the water and follows me to the gate—wish I could bring him inside the house. (Maybe I could hide him in the basement.)"

After the big meal, which was served Grandmother's style— all three courses—was finished, we all enjoyed playing games. Between the peach trees and the cherry trees there was a huge swing, and I particularly enjoyed swinging in it. The big orchard had a fence around it, and outside the fence gate, there was a lot of space where we could roam around and play freely. Inside the yard, there were beautiful flowers, and in the very corners of the backyard, there were sunflowers growing—they were so big and bright.

There was a big cottage next to the orchard where Petrovich lived, and however long before that other hired people lived there too. It was a large cottage with small windows, but always there were flower boxes full of pretty flowers planted in them. We children loved to go inside and listen to Petrovich tell us some of his fascinating stories. Next to the cottage, there was a large stable. There were no horses there anymore, and Grandmother used it to store firewood, garden tools, and whatever else had to be put away. The famous sleigh was always parked there against the back of the stable (inside), and Grandmother called it our family heirloom or ornament. It was there like it had been for many years. It was the sleigh used for our rides in the winter (and even long before our time).

That particular night, we all decided that we would sleep outside, since it was really warm that night, and the moon was so full and bright. We all dragged what bedding we could, and each one chose a place. Halina, Zina, Luci, and I decided to sleep close to the swing between two large trees. All the boys wanted to get close to the cottage and invited Petrovich to join them. There was so much laughter and noise all night long that I doubt if there was much sleep at all. I don't remember what the rest of them did after 2:00 a.m., but Halina and I decided to go back into the house, and sleep in our own beds.

This was one of the happy times when we were all together, especially since no one knew what the future was going to bring the next summer. The memories are sweet, though, like many other happy ones that I have.

CHAPTER 22

REMEMBRANCES

At this point in her transcripts, Nonna paused her story, picked up her childhood diaries, read through them, and reflected with pen. She opened to different sections and translated them just as she had written them in her childhood.

Here she mentions having written her first diary entry at the age of eight, but in every other place she says she began her diaries at age nine.

• • •

1935–36
At the Great House: Times of Uncertainty

It is one of those summer nights (sometimes in June), when the windows of the bedroom are open. My bed is near the window, and I lie there listening to all of those little noises that can be heard when the rest of the world is asleep. Somewhere near the window there is a cricket chirping away. Very faintly, but definitely, the little frogs from the near pond are singing their tunes. There is a little breeze coming from the open window, and it gently pets my face.

There is a full moon, and the little shadows from the leaves of the large trees are dancing across the wall—sort of flickering. All of that is as pleasant as a sweet lullaby. Just before I drift away into a peaceful sleep, there is just this last one thing I notice. It is a smell so sweet from the lilacs that were planted right under my window. It is the last thing which I am so aware of, and it is so enjoyable to me, as though a fragrance that was supposed to induce me into a deep sleep. For the rest of my life when I smell lilacs, I am immediately transported to that very night so many years ago. I am embraced so sweetly with the memory that it is almost as if I were there again. These memories make me feel so warm and peaceful.

• • •

1938–39
Anatoly Is Sent Away

My little heart is torn and I feel so helpless, mostly because I do not understand why these things are happening—why my brother, Anatoly, has to be sent away. I can hardly imagine what it will be like not to have him around. However, there is too much concern in my papa's eyes, and what they are all talking about makes very little sense to me. I feel so angry because I don't understand any of their plans, and I really, for the first time in my life, resent Papa's ideas. I feel so alone and helpless. No matter how hard Mama and Papa tried to talk to me and comfort me with the promise of it all being for the best for Anatoly and the rest of us, I begin to really imagine the worst.

On the days when I'd rather spend some time out of school, I would take my books, and also my music books and ice skates, to school with me. I would leave school during the big recess and make my way to my music school. Sometimes I would go across the street to the theater where Mama and I performed often. I was ballet dancing on the stage, and Mama would accompany my dancing by playing the piano. The theater would be empty (with only the keepers and the cleaning crew there). I would practice my music on the piano with the curtains up so I could see the auditorium. I thought that by doing this, I could imagine the theater was filled with people, and therefore when I had to be on the stage, I would be able to do it without paying any attention to the audience or having any stage-fright spells.

Sometimes, I would be caught by my music teacher, and she would look at me playing as she stood behind the stage. I really would get a lecture from her, and I thought that she would tell my parents about it. But she never did. However, somehow I thought later that my mama and papa knew what I was doing and just let me go on this way. After all, I was making good grades, and our private tutor made trips to our house regularly. The Russian school, and whatever was going on there, bored me extremely. We went to classes every day for eight hours, and had three recesses—two small ones for twenty-five minutes, and one long one for forty-five minutes. I would go through my tests fast, and it angered my teachers.

• • •

1939–40

It is springtime in the year 1939. The lilacs are in bloom everywhere, and the clusters are hanging over the fences near everyone's home. The entire town is filled with the magnificent aroma from the lilacs and other flowers that are in bloom. Almost everyone in town and in this village has an orchard, however small or large it may be, and some of the fruit trees are in bloom also. It is a beautiful sight that can transform one into a world of dreams and hopes.

However, there is a WAR going on! Hitler has invaded Poland. It is the worst war that our country, or the whole of Europe, has ever seen. World War II has been launched, and it is all over the continent. Hitler has decided that he has to have it all—or nothing. Life comes to a halt for almost everyone, and all the dreams and happiness that we lived for are put on hold. The Russians have cut all communications with the West and are suspicious of anyone who makes even the slightest move to contact the outside world. Grandmother dismisses all the hired hands except Petrovich. Our family is extremely worried about what the future holds.

WORLD WAR II • In August 1939, Hitler and Stalin signed a non-aggression pact dividing Poland between Germany and the Soviet Union (joined by Lithuania and Slovakia within a few months) and preventing the Soviets from defending Poland from German invasion. On September 3, Great Britain and France declared war on Germany.

Anatoly is coming home for his last visit with the family—Grandmother's brother from Riga, Latvia, is taking him home with him. The entire family is in an emotional and confused state by all that is going on. Mama is not in agreement with sending Anatoly away, but the decision had been made in order to save him from the war. Mama and Papa have many emotional outbreaks between them.

Grandmother's brother took Anatoly to Riga, and we never saw Anatoly again.

Mama was with child and was having a difficult time dealing with all the emotional stress she was under. Papa was trying to be as helpful as he knew how. These were sad times for everyone, but especially for me. I was so young, and all that I could think of was that I was unhappy over losing my brother and all the other things that were taking place in my world. Mama had a difficult pregnancy because she came down with malaria fever, which she had contracted when she and Papa went fishing and she was bitten by mosquitoes. She developed a high fever and would have bouts of this fever and have to stay in bed. There was very little medical help available, and certainly no modern medicine was available during those years.

Mama was able to carry the baby to full term, and on August 29, 1940, she gave birth to a beautiful baby girl whom she named "Taissia," in honor of her dear friend Mrs. Solzhenitsyna. However, little Taissia was born with the malaria fever, and the disease had caused liver and kidney problems. On September 3, little Taissia died, and I saw my papa cry for the first time. These were truly some of the hardest times of my life, but with my grandmother's help, I was able to overcome my sadness.

• • •

BABY TAISSIA • Nonna wrote this poem, dedicated to Anatoly, in April of 1945. Her reference to "three days" conflicts with her recollections of the baby's birth and death dates, which would have made her five days old.

BABY TAISSIA

We had a little sister, brother.
She looked so small, her eyes so blue.
Taissia, was she named by mother—
To me she was a doll, no substitute for you.

Three days had passed since she was born.
They moved her from the crib to the divan.
Our Mama stood there—her heart was torn,
Then Angels took her babe to Heaven.

Our home was filled with sorrow, brother,
And I saw Papa cry again.
You should be here to comfort Mother;
I longed to see you, though in vain.

CHAPTER 23

GERMANY ATTACKS RUSSIA

Late Summer, 1941

The last few months were full of confusion for me. I no longer liked my school and tried to find some way to skip school and stay home whenever I could manage. My grades started dropping from all A's to B's, and even some C's. Soon, Mama and Papa became very concerned and decided to move me to a Ukrainian school that was near our house, only a couple of blocks away from where we lived. However, being among strangers, with all the teaching being done in the Ukrainian language, had become a new problem for me. I took off more and more often, and spent a lot of time at my music school, dancing and practicing my piano lessons (with music—there was nothing else to hear). I also drew a lot, and spent many hours in my room reading Papa's German, Polish, and Lithuanian books. The news of the war came almost as a relief for me. There was so much sorrow and problems for everyone.

Everybody was talking about the war. The Germans are heading toward us. Whatever will become of all of us? It was a great relief for me just to not worry about school, for the time being anyway, because the schools were closed most of the time, especially after the German planes started to bomb our town regularly. Somehow I sensed that I would never have to go to that kind of school again. But all of that unknown ahead was scary in spite of whatever I was thinking.

SURPRISE ATTACK • On June 22, 1941, the Germans invaded the Soviet Union—thus breaking their ten-year nonaggression pact after only two years.

I played the piano and read constantly just to forget what was going on all around. The next few weeks were times of much confusion and fear. The German planes started bombing our town regularly, and the Russian military was moving out, taking all the civilians who wanted to be evacuated with them. The trains were loaded with people every day. The people were confused, and did not know what to do—to leave their homes and belongings and board the trains or to remain behind and face the inevitable. People with small children were the first ones to board the trains. The Russian soldiers were roaming through the streets encouraging everyone to leave. They were telling stories of much horror about what the Germans were bringing as they occupied the territories.

Papa had already decided that we would stay behind, hoping to get a chance to cross over to the other side of the border. It was our only chance to get out of Russia and move to Poland or farther west. It was a longtime dream, and now was our chance to have it come to reality. We would wait for the Germans and try to explain, hoping that they would allow Papa and us to travel to Romania or Poland—anywhere out of Russia.

Papa had planned it all for so long, he did not anticipate any problems: As soon as the first wave of troops moved out, we would deal with the German authorities, who would help us get out of the country. Papa spoke German fluently, and he counted on making them understand our plight and to help us out.

However, the Russians had other plans for the people, and that was to evacuate everybody and then bomb and dynamite everything that was left. They took all the people that wanted to be evacuated, but they also took many civilians against their will and loaded them on the last departing trains. Many of them were young children who were forced to leave their parents behind. The Russian troops were scavenging throughout the town, gathering up people to put on the trains. Petrovich, my grandmother's hired hand, was one of those. Grandmother had sent him down to get some coal that the Russians had dumped along the railroad tracks. People were picking it up and taking it to their homes when Russian soldiers rushed them and forced them to board the trains. Petrovich had left that morning, and when Grandmother missed him, she went looking for him. All she found was his cart still loaded with coal. We never saw him again.

As the Russians moved out, they burned or dynamited everything in sight. They wanted to make sure that when the Germans arrived, there would be no food or anything else left for them to find. Those of us who were left behind were of little or no concern to them, since they had labeled us as traitors anyway.

Most of those who had managed to stay behind did so by

hiding in their cellars or wherever they could find some hiding place. It was getting cold outside, and the cellars were cold and damp. Many people became sick with colds. Without medical help and little medicine, many of them died of pneumonia. We stayed in our cellar for days, getting out only at night.

The fields were mined and traps were set up just about everywhere. Now and then you could hear an explosion and then screams of someone who met his or her fate by stepping on one of those traps. The artillery could still be heard far away, especially at night, and it sounded like rolling thunder. We all knew that the fighting was going on not too far away. Occasionally, Russian planes flew over and would drop a bomb or two. There was nothing left to bomb, but they seemed to enjoy scaring those that were left behind. They would open fire on the people on the streets while they were flying over. And they flew so low that you could almost see the pilots. There was no doubt that the planes were Russian.

"THE PLANES WERE RUSSIAN" • German Luftwaffe bombings of civil-ian transports have been documented, yet Nonna was certain these bombers were Russian.

We were spending more time in the cellar than in the house itself. The frequent bombings and the searches by the Russian soldiers were keeping us hidden in the cellar for much of the time. Aunt Tonja and her two girls, Zina and Luci, and Aunt Xenja and her husband, Vladimir, decided to board a train that would take them farther into Russian-occupied territory. Aunt Tonja's husband, Alexey, was already two hundred kilometers away working as a chemist in one of the factories, and they were hoping to get there and be near him. Aunt Xenja and

Uncle Vladimir wanted to go along to protect Aunt Tonja and her young children. They planned to travel as far as Taganrog, where they would pick up Aunt Olga, who was there alone with her five children after Uncle Vanya died in a plane crash into the Azov Sea (he was flying a plane as a test pilot). Uncle Leonid was already out of town for several weeks—we did not even know where he was at that time. Uncle Zhenya and his wife, with their two very young children, were thousands of miles away in Irkutsk, where he was stationed in the air force.

Now there were only Mama, Papa, Grandmother, and myself left, since Papa had decided that we would stay behind. Grandma would never leave the Great House and would always be home in case any of her family decided to return.

CHAPTER 24

PREPARATIONS FOR THE INVASION

With the Russian troops departed and the Germans not yet there, we were all in some kind of "limbo"; everyone was wondering what was coming next. Soon we were receiving some very troublesome news from both sides. The news from the Russian side was devastating to all of us who had relatives on the last departing trains. It seemed that some of the last trains were blown up by the Russians themselves—killing all the people on them. Some of the last trains were loaded with prisoners from the Russian jails, but among those were many other civilians who were picked up by the Russian soldiers along the way. The Russians had to move fast, and they decided to blow up the trains rather than abandon them. The prisoners were of no concern to them, and the civilians had become victims of circumstance.

Since most of our relatives were on the last trains, we were hoping and praying that they were not among those who were killed. However, there was no way to know for sure, and we were absolutely devastated.

But there was news from the other side, which had become occupied by the Germans, and that news was disturbing as well. It seemed that the Germans were attacked over and over again by the Russian partisans who were scattered all around the wooded areas, and many German soldiers were killed by them. This created a lot of mistrust among the Germans—that they were not safe from any of the Russians, even those who were left behind. They started to kill anyone who looked suspicious, especially the young men and boys, but they also killed some women and old men. All of this meant one thing for us—that we had better stay hidden in our hiding places until at least the first German troops went through. The news was brought to us by some of those who had managed to escape and return to town. Needless to say, this news traveled fast throughout the town.

"NEWS FROM THE OTHER SIDE" • It is not clear what "sides" Nonna had in mind, though certainly she referred to German-occupied country.

Papa had already started to dig a tunnel from the basement of Grandmother's house to the outside cellar. His plans were to put up a fake wall from the cellar and from the basement, thereby giving him a safe place to hide. Papa was concerned about Grandmother, Mama, and me, and was trying to think of some way to protect us from the things that were yet to come. He came up with the idea that we should leave and go to the next village, where we would be safer.

STAYING BEHIND • Feodosija refused to leave the Great House. She worried that there might be looters and that German soldiers might burn down the house. She also wanted to stay at the house in case any of her children came home. At that point, Feodosija had little idea where most of her children were—and if they were alive or dead.

Since it was more dangerous on the streets for Russian men than for women, Yevgeny planned to hide in an underground tunnel and send the other three into the next village to find food and shelter.

There was plenty of food in the next village that we could offer the German soldiers, to possibly establish some sort of communication between our people and the Germans. However, Grandmother did not want to leave her home for fear that it would be ransacked or burned. She decided to stay and prepare meals for Papa while he was hiding out in the tunnel.

So, in spite of Mama's protests and tears, the decision was made for Mama to take me and go to the next village, which was at least eleven miles away. Papa promised to come for us in a short time—just long enough for the first front to go through.

"It will all work out for the best," he would say.

Grandmother was going to stay in her house, not hide in the tunnel. She said, "The worst German soldier would not want to hurt an old woman like myself."

Mama and I packed some clothes and a few other things we thought we might need in the next few days and loaded them onto a *telega* (cart), preparing for our trip. According to Papa, it would be safer for us to walk to the village in the late afternoon, or at least by dark, because he was worried about the Russian planes and what they might do if they saw us walking through the fields. It never even occurred to Papa about all those mines in the fields, but I am sure that after we left, he thought about them, too, and worried plenty. Mama thought of a way to make it through the fields by taking a sack full of large stones along with us. The idea was to roll some stones ahead of us and then follow the path where the stones had rolled. Mama would walk ahead of me, and I would follow. We were both amused by Mama's ingenuity.

In the meantime at home, Papa and Grandmother were putting the finishing touches to the tunnel. The cellar outside was built deep underground with steps leading all the way down. It was built many years ago with the purpose of storing food such as potatoes, apples, lots of barrels with pickles, sauerkraut, etc. The cellar outside the house was much cooler than the basement of the house, and Grandmother also used the outside cellar to store her homemade wine. The shelves were loaded with aged wines of all kinds. Papa had built the tunnel between the cellar and basement and, therefore, had plenty of room to hide in this tunnel.

Now they would wait, and when the first Germans came, Papa would go into his hiding place. It should be only for a day or two. The worst that was expected from the German troops was that they would search the empty houses for food—they would not take any chances if there were people in the houses.

HOME INVASION • The German soldiers came through Russia unprepared for a long battle. They, too, faced starvation, and they ransacked houses searching for something to eat. They killed anyone who got in their way. Papa had been too optimistic when he thought he might reason with the young German soldiers, even though he spoke the German language.

Mama and I were making our journey through the fields, and Mama's idea of rolling the stones ahead of us was working out very well. However, it was getting dark outside, and it was hard to see where the stones were rolling. It was also very time consuming, and it began to look like we would be walking all night long. We were both very tired and hungry but did not dare to stop and rest. We tried to stay in the middle of the fields and not get too close to the wooded area for fear that there were partisans in the woods who could make us join them. We told riddles and sang songs quietly as we were walking, which made us both feel better and kept us from getting too sleepy. It must have been close to midnight when we finally reached the village. We stopped at the first farmhouse and asked the people if we could spend the night there.

The farmer and his wife were very compassionate to us after Mama told them our story. Their house was full of people, and there were several small children scattered all around on blankets on the floor of the room we had entered. Mama asked the farmer if we could stay in his barn and use some straw for our bed, and he was only too happy to accommodate Mama's request. The barn was very large, there was plenty of straw, and the barn was quite warm, too. The woman of the house had brought us some fresh-baked bread and some milk, which made us feel very welcome. It had been a long time since I had such good-tasting bread, and I ate most of it myself, leaving Mama with the milk.

As we lay there on the straw, looking out of the barn opening, we could see how brightly the moon was shining. We did not have such a bright moon to accompany us as we were walking just a few hours earlier. For just a few short minutes, we forgot all about the war and the killings that were happening all around us, and we were asleep in no time at all.

THE SERENKOVS • Nonna never forgot the farmer's family and kept a photograph of a couple whom she identified as the Serenkovs with her throughout the war. The photograph has also survived.

CHAPTER 25

OUR WORLD BEGINS
TO CRUMBLE

Fall 1941

When Mama and I woke up, it was daylight, and we heard the farmer's wife coming down to the barn. She greeted us and asked us if we had rested well, and indeed Mama and I had gotten a good night's sleep. However, when we opened our eyes, the first thing to enter our minds was Papa and Grandmother, whom we had left behind. The farmer's wife invited us to come to the house and have breakfast with the family. She had pancakes with sour cream and had homemade preserves. This was a meal fit for a king, and Mama and I both enjoyed the breakfast. After we had finished eating, Mama was asking her if there was a place where we could stay for a couple of days or until Papa would come for us. The lady pointed to a few houses in the village and assured Mama that there were many empty houses around that were left unattended when the Russians evacuated the people. Those being evacuated had just taken a few clothes and small things that they could take with them. The lady told Mama that she could look around and find a place to stay for a few days in one of those houses.

Mama and I went looking for someplace that we thought would be safe and yet not be too far away from other people. We looked at several houses that day, and selected this farmhouse where there were some livestock that had been left unattended. Even having animals around gave us a little sense of not being alone, and we could feed the livestock while we were there. The house that we selected was a typical farmhouse that had a nice little kitchen, bedrooms, and a parlor with a big fireplace. The amazing thing was how clean and neat the owners had left everything when they evacuated. The beds had sheets and pillows, and to look at the place, one would think that the owners could return at any time. Mama and I went back to the farmer's house where we had spent the night and told the family that we were going to stay at the place we had found. Both the farmer and his wife told us that if we needed anything to come tell them and they would help us in any way they could.

Food was no problem, because there were potatoes and carrots still in the ground in the fields, and all one had to do was go out and gather what was needed. However, by this time, there were German soldiers marching through the area, and Mama and I decided that we would stay close to the house and act as if it were our home. The main problem was that there was no bread, and by that time no mills were operating to provide the flour that was needed to make bread. However, Mama invented a way to grind the wheat when she found two tin buckets where one fit inside the other. She took a nail, and drove nail holes into the outer bucket which would leave sharp "teeth" inside the bucket's bottom. She drove as many nail holes as she could in the bottom of the bucket, and then drove nail holes from the inside of the other bucket, which would leave the nail holes pointing out. These nail holes in effect left sharp teeth that would sit pointing toward the teeth of the other bucket—thus creating a kind of grinder to use on the grain.

There was no shortage of wheat, but the grain bins had been dynamited by the Russians when they evacuated. The wheat was full of glass and debris from the dynamiting, so we had to figure out a way to separate the grains of wheat from the glass and debris. There was only one way, and that was to sit at the table and sort the wheat from the glass and debris—one grain at a time. This was tedious work, and very time consuming, but it kept our mind occupied and helped to pass the time. When we would get enough wheat kernels sorted, we would put them into the outer bucket. Mama had rigged up a handle on the inner bucket so we could turn it. The teeth she had created by driving the nail holes in the bucket would slowly grind the wheat into a coarse type of meal. Mama would then boil the wheat meal and make a type of porridge, but we had to cook it several hours before it would be tender enough to eat.

We would spend several hours each day cleaning the wheat to make a substitute for bread, and we would go out and gather firewood to use in the stove. When we needed potatoes, we would ask the farmer if we could dig enough for that day. People were kind and willing to help each other in any way that they could. They would share whatever they had because of the uncertain times—everyone was unsure as to what tomorrow would bring.

The first few days seemed to pass rather quickly as we established a pattern and oriented ourselves to the surroundings. Mama looked worried and unhappy, but she tried to hide her concerns from me by singing songs and trying to keep busy doing something—anything to stay busy. When we felt it was safe, we would walk to the farmer's house, and Mama and the lady would talk about the war and how scared everyone was. Mama would mention Papa and hoped that he would be safe until we returned.

There were a lot of German soldiers around the village and on the roads. They did not bother us but would give us curious looks when they would see us. After a few more days, the concerns about the soldiers subsided, but Mama and I kept as far away from them as possible. The weather was beginning to turn cold, but we were able to stay warm enough and spent more and more time inside the house. With each passing day, Mama's concern grew stronger because we had not heard from Papa. Mama told me that there were too many soldiers in the area for Papa to be outside, and she was worried about him being in hiding in the tunnel with the weather becoming so much colder. It seemed that we had been there for a long time, but it was only about two weeks since we had left Papa and Grandmother in Konstantinowka at the Great House. We were both sad and missing our family.

Anatoly, Nonna, Anna, and Yevgeny pose in 1935 for a family photo—likely the last taken before Anatoly left for school in St. Petersburg.

Nonna at age three, holding her favorite doll.

Nonna at age eight, wearing a hairstyle typical of young girls during this time.

Nonna's mother, Anna Yakovlevna Ljaschova.

Nonna's parents, Anna and Yevgeny.

Nonna's father, Yevgeny Ivanovich Lisowsky, was from Warsaw, Poland. (ca. 1937)

Nonna's parents, Anna and Yevgeny. Anna, pregnant with Taissia, is standing on rocks to appear taller and slimmer.

Anatoly at about three years of age. (ca. 1928)

Nonna and Anatoly, dressed in warm clothing during the frigid Russian winter.

Anatoly during his last visit home. (ca. 1938)

Each year the family gathered at the Great House for their traditional wine tasting. Feodosija made wine from the cherries that grew in the orchard. Pictured here are Uncle Ivan (son Dimitry in his lap), Feodosija, Anna, Uncle Vladimir, Aunt Xenja, Aunt Tonja (daughter Luci in her lap).

One of the family's grain mills. Nonna's maternal grandparents, Yakov and Feodosija, owned seven grain mills located in the Ukraine and southern Russia. The family kept houses, or *dachas*, at each mill.

Nonna's maternal grandfather, Yakov Sergeyevich Ljaschov, was a Cossack and a friend of Nicholas II, the last Tzar of Russia. This was a birthday card to him from the Tzar.

Petrovich was the caretaker of the Great House, near Konstantinowka. All the grandchildren loved him, as he was never too busy to take them riding in the sleigh or participate in their activities.

Feodosija Nikolayevna Ljaschova was Nonna's maternal grandmother and Anna's mother. Feodosija taught her daughter and granddaughter to love God.

THIS SIDE IS FOR PERSONS MAKING CLAIMS FOR BANK ACCOUNTS
Current Name: _NONNA L. BANNISTER_   Name (In Europe): _NONNA L. BANNISTER_
Current Address: _MEMPHIS, TN 38115_
Current Tel. #: ~~_____~~   Fax #: ~~_____~~
Father's Name: _YEVGENY LISOWSKIJ_   Mother's Name: _ANNA LJASCHOVA_
Brothers' Names: (If Alive Please Include Present Address & Phone Numbers)
ANATOLY JEVGENEVITCH LISOWSKIJ - FATHER SENT HIM TO LIVE
WITH RELATIVES IN LATVIA. I NEVER SAW HIM AGAIN
Sisters' Names: (If Alive Please Include Present Address & Phone Numbers)
TAISSA EVGENYINA LISOWSKAJA - DIED AT THREE DAYS OLD.

Names - Maternal Relatives with relationship (use extra sheets if needed):
SEE EXHIBIT I - MATERNAL RELATIVES

Names - Paternal Relatives with relationship (use extra sheets if needed):
SEE EXHIBIT II - PATERNAL RELATIVES

Villages/Cities Family Was From in Europe: _SEE EXHIBIT III_

Ghettos/Concentration Camps Interned in and the Periods of Internment:
SEE EXHIBIT IV
Concentration Camp Numbers for you and all living relatives: (Include each persons name
with the number only - if you know the information)
MOTHER'S KZ # 23993 - WAS CHANGED TO 52234 BEFORE BURNED TO DEATH
Red Cross and/or Refugee Card Numbers for you and all living relatives: (Include each
persons name with the number - only if you know the information)
UNKNOWN FOR MOTHER - NONNA LISKOWSKAJA Displaced Person #56531
Families Occupation in Europe:
How do you know or why do you believe Monies Were Put Into Swiss Banks: _INFORMATION_
THAT WAS TOLD TO ME BY MY GRANDMOTHER ABOUT GRANDFATHER'S
MONEY BEING SENT TO A "FOREIGN" BANK FOR SAFETY.
Efforts previously taken to get back monies from Swiss Banks or the Ombudsman's Office:
NONE

[Describe on separate paper and attach copies of documents used in attempts to get monies]
How much money you believe was deposited into Banks, by which relatives & in which Banks?
UNKNOWN
Do you have photographs showing (Family members,) other persons (who later survived) and
Home taken before internment? _YES_ If so, may we have copies for our files? _YES_
Your Present Age and are you in good health? _72 YRS OLD - VERY POOR HEALTH_

Signed: _Nonna L. Bannister_   Dated: _January 1998_

Preliminary questionnaire for Holocaust survivors or
their heirs.

Country / Land		Since when / seit wann
RUSSIA		1941

Period of persecution: / Aufenthalt während der Verfolgung:

Type of persecution (KZ, Ghetto, life in hiding, life under conditions resembling imprisonment) Please state precisely: / Art der Verfolgung (KZ, Ghetto, versteckt gelebt, Leben unter haftähnlichen Bedingungen) bitte genau angeben:	Place of persecution within the indicated time periods: / Ort der Verfolgung im genannten Zeitabschnitt:
Nazis severely beat my father after finding him in hiding. My father died from the beating.	Konstantinowka Russia
Mother and I were taken to Germany on the cattle trains for forced labor camps.	Kassel; Lichtenau; back to Kassel and then to Marienkrankenhaus.
Gestapo "arrested" mother and sent her to concentration camp in Ravensbruk. She was moved to several different camps and ended up in Flossenberg. She was thrown into the incinerator in 1945.	Ravensbruk Buchenwald Treblinka Flossenberg
Catholic Nuns and Priests hid me and changed my name to Lena Shutz to save my life.	Marienkrankenhaus Germany
I spent this time looking for my mother in Merxhausen. I moved to Hersfeld, Germany.	1948 1950
I immigrated to America arriving in New Orleans, LA in June 1950.	May 1950 Now

5. All countries of residence after persecution until today: / Alle Wohnländer nach der Verfolgung bis heute:

Country / Land	From / von	To / bis
Germany	1942	1950
America	1950	Present

"Where were you during your period of persecution? Type of
persecution? Please state precisely."

Patches were required to be worn by all prisoners, victims including children.

The Patches Had To be stitched on clothing

Jews
[left arm or left side on chest]

Russians Ukrainians
on the left side of chest

←East→

Poles
[Right side of chest or Right Arm]

Nonna drew these patches, depicting the ones that Jews, Russians, and Poles were required to wear.

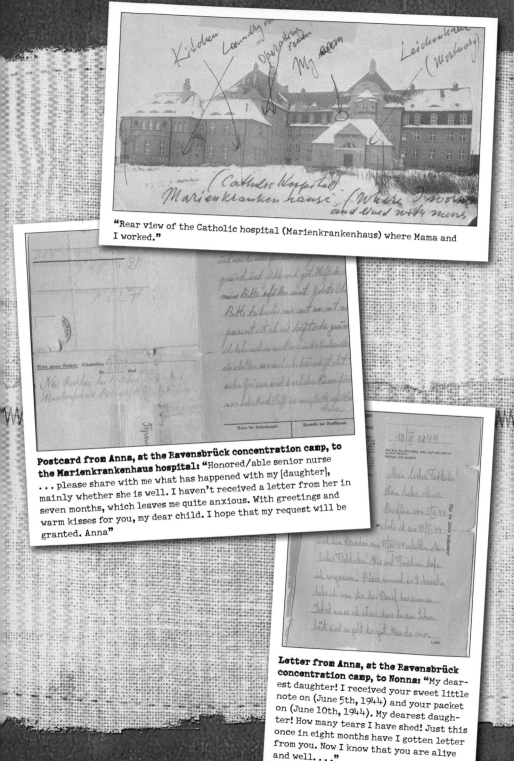

"Rear view of the Catholic hospital (Marienkrankenhaus) where Mama and I worked."

Postcard from Anna, at the Ravensbrück concentration camp, to the Marienkrankenhaus hospital: "Honored/able senior nurse ... please share with me what has happened with my [daughter], mainly whether she is well. I haven't received a letter from her in seven months, which leaves me quite anxious. With greetings and warm kisses for you, my dear child. I hope that my request will be granted. Anna"

Letter from Anna, at the Ravensbrück concentration camp, to Nonna: "My dearest daughter! I received your sweet little note on (June 5th, 1944) and your packet on (June 10th, 1944). My dearest daughter! How many tears I have shed! Just this once in eight months have I gotten letter from you. Now I know that you are alive and well...."

Marienkrankenhaus Hospital

A group of nurses gather for a photo. Nonna is in the back row, second from the right.

Nonna became a patient in the hospital where she worked. She is pictured in the back, with braids, along with "another patient (center), a nurse from Yugoslavia on the left, and a nurse from Russia on the right."

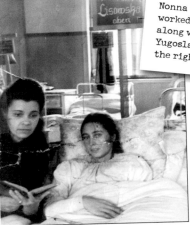

Nonna recovered from rheumatic fever at the Marienkrankenhaus Catholic Hospital in Kassel, Germany. Note Nonna's name on the sign above her bed. (ca. 1945)

Menschenwachen kann nichts nützen,
Gott muss wachen, Gott muss schützen.
Herr, durch deine Güt' und Macht
gib uns eine gute Nacht!

Hört, ihr Herrn, und lasst euch sagen:
unsre Glock hat zwölf geschlagen!
Zwölf, das ist das Ziel der Zeit;
Mensch, bedenk die Ewigkeit!
Menschenwachen kann nichts nützen,
Gott muss wachen, Gott muss schützen.
Herr, durch deine Güt' und Macht
gib uns eine gute Nacht!

Hört, ihr Herrn, und lasst euch sagen:
unsre Glock hat eins geschlagen!
Eins ist allein der ewige Gott,
der uns helf aus aller Not!

A poem written by Nonna in her post-war diary:

Watch-keeping will accomplish naught;
God holds vigil, God must protect.
Lord, through your goodness and strength
We ask you give us a good night. . . .

Listen, you men, let yourselves be told:
On o'clock our bell has tolled!
The eternal God alone is one,
Our sole aid in all distress!

Nonna and her friend Alvina in their nursing uniforms, in front of a German truck.

Nonna and her friend Zoya, who helped her apply for a visa. (Butzbach, 1950)

Another of Nonna's poems:

All the starlets disappear,
And the day will soon appear.
Thanks to God, who through the night
Such fatherly protection us has given!

"I am finally leaving the land of many horrors to make a new life for myself in the land of freedom—America. Here I am, standing on the bow of the *General Haan* as we set sail!"

Nonna and Henry are married at his parents' home in Baton Rouge, Louisiana. (June 23, 1951)

THE UNITED STATES OF AMERICA

ORIGINAL
TO BE GIVEN TO
THE PERSON NATURALIZED

CERTIFICATE OF

No. 7140281

NATURALIZATION

Petition No. 822

Personal description of holder as of date of naturalization: Date of birth September 22, 1925 sex female
complexion light color of eyes blue color of hair brown height 5 feet 4 inches;
weight 100 pounds; visible distinctive marks none
Marital status married

I certify that the description above given is true, and that the photograph affixed hereto is a likeness of me.

Nonna Lisowskaja Bannister
(Complete and true signature of holder)

State of Louisiana
Parish E. Baton Rouge } ss:

Be it known that at a term of the United States District Court of
Eastern District of Louisiana
held pursuant to law at Baton Rouge, Louisiana
on April 14, 1953 the Court having found that
Nonna Lisowskaja Bannister
then residing at _____, Baton Rouge, Louisiana
intends to reside permanently in the United States (when so required by the
Naturalization Laws of the United States) had in all other respects complied with
the applicable provisions of such naturalization laws, and was entitled to be
admitted to citizenship, thereupon ordered that such person be and she was
admitted as a citizen of the United States of America.

In testimony whereof the seal of the court is hereunto affixed this 14th
day of April in the year of our Lord nineteen hundred and
fifty-three and of our Independence the one hundred
and seventy-seventh.

A. DALLAM O'BRIEN, JR.
Clerk of the United States Dist. Court.

By Nelson B. Jones Deputy Clerk.

It is a violation of the U.S. Code (and
punishable as such) to copy, print, photograph,
or otherwise illegally use this certificate.

DEPARTMENT OF JUSTICE

Nonna's certificate of naturalization.

Nonna with her children: Hank, Elizabeth, and John. (1960)

Nonna at the piano. (December 14, 1994)

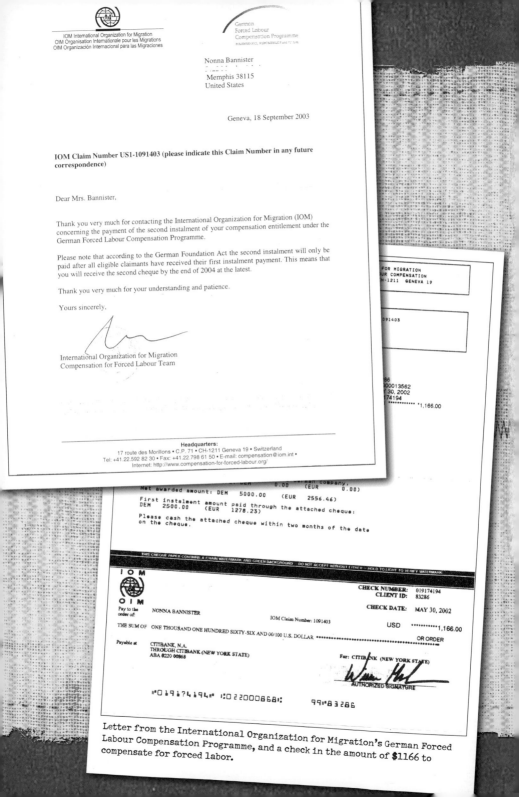

IOM International Organization for Migration
OIM Organisation Internationale pour les Migrations
OIM Organización Internacional para las Migraciones

German
Forced Labour
Compensation Programme

Nonna Bannister
Memphis 38115
United States

Geneva, 18 September 2003

IOM Claim Number US1-1091403 (please indicate this Claim Number in any future correspondence)

Dear Mrs. Bannister,

Thank you very much for contacting the International Organization for Migration (IOM) concerning the payment of the second instalment of your compensation entitlement under the German Forced Labour Compensation Programme.

Please note that according to the German Foundation Act the second instalment will only be paid after all eligible claimants have received their first instalment payment. This means that you will receive the second cheque by the end of 2004 at the latest.

Thank you very much for your understanding and patience.

Yours sincerely,

International Organization for Migration
Compensation for Forced Labour Team

Net awarded amount: DEM 5000.00 (EUR 0.00)
First instalment amount paid through the attached cheque:
DEM 2500.00 (EUR 1278.23)
Please cash the attached cheque within two months of the date on the cheque.

THIS CHEQUE PAPER CONTAINS A CHAIN WATERMARK AND GREEN BACKGROUND DO NOT ACCEPT WITHOUT EITHER – HOLD TO LIGHT TO VERIFY WATERMARK

IOM
OIM

CHECK NUMBER: 619174194
CLIENT ID: 83286

CHECK DATE: MAY 30, 2002

Pay to the order of: NONNA BANNISTER

IOM Claim Number: 1091403

USD **********1,166.00

THE SUM OF ONE THOUSAND ONE HUNDRED SIXTY-SIX AND 00/100 U.S. DOLLAR ****************

OR ORDER

Payable at CITIBANK, N.A.
THROUGH CITIBANK (NEW YORK STATE)
ABA 0220 00868

For: CITIBANK (NEW YORK STATE)

AUTHORIZED SIGNATURE

⑆019174194⑆ ⑈022000868⑈ 99⑈83286

Letter from the International Organization for Migration's German Forced Labour Compensation Programme, and a check in the amount of $1166 to compensate for forced labor.

CHAPTER 26

Papa Is Found in Hiding

One day a man from Grandmother's neighborhood came looking for Mama and told her that she needed to go back home because her husband had been hurt very badly. He didn't tell Mama how he was hurt or how badly but told her that she should go immediately because my grandmother needed her. Mama was really concerned and told me that she must go and check on things at home. She told me that I could stay with the farmer and his family. With that, she took me to the farmer's house and asked the lady if I could stay with her while she went to check on things at home. The lady quickly agreed and asked Mama if she needed any help. Mama told her no and left immediately. I was scared and felt very lonely and uncomfortable being left alone with strangers. The children seemed so different from me, and they would look at me in funny ways. I didn't sleep that night, but rather lay there crying and wondering what was going on with Papa and Grandmother.

The next day, Mama and Grandmother came back pulling a telega, with Papa inside the telega all covered with blankets. When I ran out to see him, I was horrified at what I saw. Papa was lying there with both eyes missing, and his head was so swollen that I hardly recognized him. The farmer's wife was telling my mother to bring Papa into their house and for us to stay there, and she would help us with Papa. Mama agreed to accept her offer, and we took Papa inside the house where the lady prepared a bed for him. However, Papa was conscious, and he called me over to his bed. Even though he could not see me, he told me not to worry, that he was going to be all right now that he had Mama and me with him. I knew he must have been in awful pain. But he tried not to show how much pain he was having.

The next few days were just a blur for me. I didn't want to leave Papa's side, and my little heart was broken.

NONNA AND PAPA • Nonna deeply loved her father. She described Yevgeny as "very strict in teaching me the values that only a father who deeply loves his child would be so intent on teaching." She remembered "some small surprises" Yevgeny hid in his pockets for Nonna whenever he came home from a trip. By age four, Nonna had learned Polish and German from her father. "I knew my ABCs in three languages, and I could scribble many words in those languages."

Mama and the lady would put cold cloths on Papa's head and sponged him down to try to make him more comfortable. He seemed to perk up a little bit and was able to sit in a chair by the kitchen table for a while each day. Everyone was concerned that the German soldiers might come in and find Papa there—and finish killing him. So when we heard the soldiers or they would come close to the house, we would hide Papa in a closet until they moved on.

Grandmother told us how she had found Papa in the cellar, beaten and bleeding, when she had taken him some food to eat. When Grandmother found Papa, the drunken German soldiers had already left and probably thought Papa was dead—not that they cared. Papa was able to tell us that he had caught a cold while he was hiding in the tunnel because it was cold and damp and there was no heat. Papa had heard the German soldiers in the cellar eating and drinking Grandmother's wine. The soldiers had been in the cellar for quite a while—long enough to get drunk—and they were cursing and singing and making a lot of noise. Papa had stayed quietly in the tunnel. He was safe until he had to cough. The German soldiers heard him cough and began to look for him and found him hiding in the tunnel. Papa told us that he had tried to reason with them, but they savagely beat him and left him for dead.

PAPA'S CONDITION • It is not clear why Yevgeny needed to go into hiding, nor why he was beaten once discovered. Perhaps a Soviet man in hiding was simply suspect.

Grandmother decided to return home, since she was not able to be of help here, and the house was crowded anyway. She decided that she would go back to the Great House to try to protect what little she had left and also to keep the looters away.

Grandmother told Mama to send for her if she needed help, so Grandmother left, and Mama and I stayed by Papa's side at all times. Occasionally, Mama would go into the next room and I would hear her crying, but she was trying to put on a good face for me. However, I was aware of how badly Papa was beaten, and how much he must have been suffering. After we were there about ten days, Mama decided that we would be better off if we found a place of our own, so as not to impose on these people any longer.

MOVING ON • Although they were already in a separate house from the Serenkov family, Anna must have felt their dependence on them was an imposition.

Feodosija decided to return to the Great House in spite of the dangerous journey back to Konstantinowka and the chaos and potential danger of living in the house once she got there. She was intensely dedicated to protecting the house, even at the risk of her own life.

The next day Mama told me to stay with Papa, that she was going to look for another place for us to move to. She was gone most of the morning. When she returned, she told us she had found a place that would be better for us, and it would be even closer to Grandmother's house (about three miles closer). The farmer and his wife helped Mama move Papa into the telega, and we walked to our new home.

"THREE MILES CLOSER" • According to Nonna's later note, the new house was probably more like eight miles closer to the Great House than where they had been before—only three miles away from it.

It was a large house with a big foyer and several large rooms, even though it looked more like an office building or a post office than it did a home. Mama got Papa situated in the bed, and we started a fire in the stove to warm up the room. Mama put on a pot of potatoes to cook, along with some of the wheat flour that we had prepared—it seemed to me that she kept those two things cooking at all times. We settled down to try to make Papa as comfortable as possible. Papa was still very calm and talked to Mama and me, telling us not to be bitter at the Germans—that they were doing what they had been told to do.

He kept assuring Mama not to worry, saying, "I am going to be okay. I am strong, and I will be fine, especially since I have you and Nonna here with me."

Papa was mentally alert, and as usual, he was very calm and almost peaceful as we were trying to take care of him, but you could see that he was getting weaker with the passing of each day. He had developed a cough. He would have coughing spells and would cough up blood, then the coughing would subside.

Amazingly, through the whole ordeal, as horrible as it was for Papa, he had remained the same gentle and kind person he had always been. For him, there was always a reason for any situation (no matter how horrible it was), and he would forgive anyone for what was done to him. At times it would infuriate me the way he would defend the actions of those who had so unjustly hurt him.

"They could not help themselves and did what they did to protect themselves from the unknown," Papa would say.

To me, it was a simple act of cruelty and sadism. Papa kept emphasizing how important it was for me to keep practicing my German language until I could speak it fluently. Papa had written poems in many languages, and he loved to recite poems in all the languages that he spoke—he spoke eight languages. Even as he lay there so very ill, he kept teaching me how to pronounce some of the words that were difficult for me. He also recited German poems to me, and he was always telling me how important it was to learn more than two languages. (I already spoke four languages—Russian, Ukrainian, Yiddish, and Polish.)

One morning after we woke up, Mama fixed some breakfast and helped Papa into a chair by the table. Papa was quiet and would reach up and put his hand on his forehead. I am sure that he was in pain, but he never complained—not even one time. Mama was trying to get him to eat some food, but he said he wasn't hungry. As we were sitting there, Papa said, "I would give anything in the world for a piece of bacon and a glass of buttermilk. I can just taste the bacon, and that is all I'm hungry for."

I got up, put on my coat and hat, and told Mama that I was going to look for some bacon and buttermilk for Papa. I put on my shawl and wrapped up as best I could because it was very cold outside. I set out for the farmer's house where we had stayed. I saw a few German soldiers, but I walked at a fast pace and made out like I didn't see them, and they did not say anything to me.

When I arrived at the farmer's house, I told the lady that Papa was dying and that he wanted some bacon and some buttermilk for his breakfast. The lady said, "No problem, my child," and she went into the pantry and came out with a large hunk of slab bacon. She then poured a gallon of buttermilk into a jug and put them into the sack I had brought with me. She put in some potatoes and carrots and asked me if we needed any help with Papa. I told her that we were doing okay and that Mama and I were doing all we could for Papa. I thanked her and told her I didn't have any money to pay her with. She told me not to worry about it, but if I would bring her an umbrella when I came again, she would be very thankful.

I felt so very happy and proud that I had found what Papa had asked for, and my little feet couldn't carry me fast enough to get me back home. Again, there were German soldiers on the road, but I hid the sack under my shawl and kept moving toward home. When I got home with the little sack, Mama was amazed that I had found the bacon and the buttermilk, and she quickly sliced some of the bacon into bite-size cubes and fried it for Papa. She poured a glass of buttermilk and gave it to Papa as he was sitting at the table. I could see a smile come across his face as the smell of the bacon wafted through the kitchen. When Mama put the bacon on a plate and set it in front of Papa, he smiled and said, "I know that I don't have to worry about anything when my little girl, Nonna, is here to take care of us."

As he sat there eating the bacon, he seemed so happy and looked like he was enjoying it so much. Mama and I both had tears in our eyes. Papa was telling Mama and me to eat some of the bacon with him, but though it smelled so good, Mama and I would not eat any of it because we wanted to save it for Papa. After he finished eating, he looked so relaxed. He told us he felt like taking a nap, so Mama and I helped him back to the bed. He was soon asleep, and Mama and I were sitting quietly talking about the situation that we were in and that Papa was not getting any better.

There was a knock, and when I went to answer the door, there was an old man standing there. He said he was a doctor. He had heard we had an injured person there, and he would like to see if he could help out. Mama had come to the door, and she let the man come in and check on Papa.

After he had checked Papa over, he just shook his head and

said it was too late to help Papa—it would be only a matter of time before Papa would die. He apologized for not being able to help Papa, but there was no medicine available. But he took five small pills out of his coat pocket and told Mama they would help some with the pain. The old man smelled the bacon and said he was hungry, so Mama asked him to have lunch with us. He then told us that he was helping the German doctors at the field hospital and that he was obligated to get back to work at the hospital.

After the old man left, Papa asked me to go visit the neighbors' children for a while because he wanted to talk to Mama alone. I reluctantly dressed and went to the neighbors' house, and visited there for a few hours. In my heart, I knew that Papa and Mama were discussing plans for Mama and me after Papa was gone. Papa was such an intelligent man. His concerns were for Mama and me, and he was worried about what would happen to us after he was gone. When I went home, Papa was lying in the bed, and he seemed to be at peace. Mama was sitting there holding his hand, and she had her arm around his shoulders. My mind went back to Anatoly, and I was wishing he was there with us—I kept hoping he would just appear and be there for us—but it was not to be. We went to bed that night, and I could hear Mama softly crying. After a long time, I drifted off to sleep—not knowing what tomorrow would bring.

CHAPTER 27

MY LAST MINUTES
WITH PAPA

The six weeks that Papa lay there fighting to stay alive seemed like an eternity! I had held on to the hope that I would see my brother, Anatoly, again—but thoughts that were horrifying to me would go through my head at times. I would think that if Anatoly were there, he, too, could be beaten by the German soldiers, and we could lose him as well! Some nights I would just lie there in my bed and imagine all kinds of terrible things (at the age of fourteen, my imagination was quite active, anyway). I was no longer a child, but not yet a woman—however, my thoughts were too mature for my age!

The next morning Mama came to my bed and woke me, saying, "Nonnatchka, I must go now and get Grandmother. It is time, and we need her here with us."

Then she said in a very calm and quiet voice, "You sit by

Papa's bed. Don't be frightened, but just don't leave him alone. He is quiet now, and you don't need to do anything for him, but just sit there with him until I return." Somehow, I knew that things did not look very good for Papa, and I did what Mama had instructed me to do—I went to sit with Papa.

It would be at least an hour before Mama would come back, since she had to walk to Grandmother's house, which was at least four *versts* away (one verst equals three-quarters of a mile). Mama had moved Papa's bed into the kitchen because it was the only room in the house that was warm enough for him. A good fire was burning in the stove, and it was nice and warm there. Papa lay very quietly, and I thought he was asleep.

I sat for a long time just watching Papa, when suddenly an incredibly peaceful feeling came over me. It was almost as though I was surrounded by a dozen angels or something. I looked at Papa, and I saw an expression on his face that was not there a few minutes before—he looked as though he smiled. His lips were not moving, but I thought I heard him say, "It is all right now, and I am happy." I leaned over closer to his face and whispered, "Papa, are you awake?" But there was no motion, and for the first time, I noticed that his chest was not moving. I stood up and slowly started to walk backward without taking my eyes off of Papa until I was out of the kitchen. I felt like I needed some fresh air. I ran outside without my cap or coat, and I started walking around a small tree in the deep snow. I kept going in circles, and I kept chanting, "Papa is happy! Papa is happy!" My little body was freezing, but I didn't want to go inside the house.

What finally snapped me out of my shock was the sound of a motorcycle coming through the gate. There were two German soldiers on it; they jumped off the motorcycle and ran to the front door. They kicked the door open and ran inside the house. I followed them because I didn't want Papa to be alone with them, and one of them started to shout, *"Kartoffeln, Kartoffeln und Brot!"* ("Potatoes, potatoes and bread—where do you keep it?")

Before I could say anything, they started to turn everything upside down and were running from one room to another, turning the mattresses and the furniture over. I just stood there terrified—not knowing what to say or what to do. When they got to the kitchen and saw Papa there, they stopped short and looked very startled. They had the look on their faces of wild animals that were ready to attack their prey.

Filled with horror, I cried, *"Er ist mein Vater, und er ist tot!"* ("He is my father, and he is dead!") At that time, I saw one of the soldiers going for his knife and yelling, "It is a Russian trick to play dead! Let's see how dead he is!"

Like a bolt of lightning a horrible thought hit me: *What if Papa was not yet dead and was just unconscious?* I started to pray out loud, "Please, God, let Papa be dead!" Swiftly, the German soldier pulled his knife out of its holster and plunged it into Papa's chest. The other soldier grabbed him by his arm and pulled him away from Papa, yelling, "Let's go. She is telling the truth—he is dead!"

They stormed out of the kitchen, pushing me against the wall. Bewildered and in shock, I stood there against that wall shaking violently until my knees gave out and I slid down the wall. I stayed that way—just shaking—I could not move nor cry. Then I saw black boots before me, and I looked up—one of the soldiers had come back. He stared at me for a minute or so and said, "You speak German very well; where is the rest of your family?"

Thinking that he had come back to kill someone, I was

hoping that Mama and Grandmother would not come home just then. I said very quickly, "They are all dead!"

He walked back into the kitchen and came back out carrying a pot of potatoes that Mama had cooked the night before—he must have spotted the pot when they were in the kitchen.

He looked at me, and I thought that he looked kind of sad. I almost felt sorry for him! He said, "I am sorry, but we are very hungry and very cold." With this, he took off, and I remained on my knees absolutely terrified and unable to move.

When Mama and Grandmother finally walked in, I started to cry uncontrollably! Grandmother put her shawl around me, and the three of us stood there for a long time, just sobbing.

IN MEMORY OF PAPA • "Papa's love, affection, and protection stayed with me until I lost him," Nonna wrote in her transcripts. "I was at his bedside when he died. I could not believe that it was really happening. Papa taught me many things during my first fourteen years of life, but he never knew what the war and the Holocaust would bring on all of us. I thank God for those years that I had with my loving father, and I thank Papa for all that he taught me."

At this point in her transcript, Nonna included one of her father's favorite sayings, along with a poem she wrote to him after his death.

"There was no shame in those who had committed an execution where there had been no crime!"

TO PAPA

With tears in your eyes, you've softly spoken,
"We shall remain and take a chance.
Though others had been treated roughly,
We'll beg—to give us some defense!"
Now was our chance to cross the borders,

And with a smile so sweet, you'd say,
"We must believe and look for rainbows—
The freedom was just miles away."
But when the troops arrived so swiftly,
There was no time to talk—just hide.
You've waited days in the cellar (sickly),
Then the Germans found you inside.
You tried to tell them, give them the reason;
They were too drunk to understand—
For them it was a hunting season,
Of those still in the land!
With terror in my heart I've cried,
"*Er ist mein Vater, und er ist tot!*"
But faces froze and filled with spite,
Of those without respect for God.
There were no lilies on your coffin;
Your hands were folded on your chest.
I could not cry, but stood there hoping
Your soul was free and you could rest.
They tortured you while you were living,
And pierced your heart when you lay dead.
You've taught me how to be forgiving,
Please tell me how to forget!

CHAPTER 28

PAPA'S BURIAL

We were grief stricken, and so alone, and so helpless! However, there were some arrangements that had to be made, and Papa had to be buried. While Mama and I had to find someone to build a coffin for Papa, Grandmother went back to her house to look for help from her neighbors there.

Mama and I walked around for hours asking people if there was anyone who could help us. Finally, we came to a place where there was a lumber storage, and we heard some nailing going on inside. There were three older men building something. Mama asked them if they could make a coffin for Papa, and with a compassionate look in their aged eyes, they agreed to do it. They told us to come back in three hours, and they would have the coffin ready by then. When we came back and I saw the coffin they had built, I could not imagine Papa being buried in it—it was so plain, and not even painted. The old men apologized to us for not having any paint, but we knew that they had done the best they could do under the circumstances. We were grateful for what they had done. They would not even allow us to pay them for their work on the coffin—money did not mean anything to anyone then, anyway. They wanted to know how Mama and I would manage to get the coffin to our house, since it was at least one and a half miles away. There was no way to get it back home except for Mama and me to carry it.

When we made it back to the house with the coffin, Grandmother was there with several men and women whom she had gathered from around her neighborhood. I wanted to just disappear and not be there for the rest of it—so I went back to my room and closed the door behind me. I don't know how long I remained in my room with my face covered with a pillow. I lay there on my bed, filled with grief and anger, and I didn't know whom I was angry with the most—the Russians, the Germans, the war itself, or the whole world that we were living in. I could feel myself clenching my teeth until my jaws hurt. I could no longer cry—my eyes were dry, and no matter how hard I tried to cry, I just could not cry. I felt as though I were slowly being crushed by the heavy air and the atmosphere around me.

Then I heard the wailing of the women coming from the parlor where Papa's coffin was placed. It was a custom that the Russians and the Ukrainians practiced before burying the dead. It was as gruesome a sound as anyone could ever hear. I could no longer stand the sound that they were making and stuck my fingers in both my ears. I ran out of my room, passing the parlor, and into the yard. The cold air felt good to me, and I took a handful of snow and rubbed it all over my face until it burned and hurt.

Someone had found a horse and buggy; it was there by the gate waiting for Papa's coffin to be loaded onto it. Grandmother took my hand, and we walked to the next house (our neighbors'). She asked the lady if I could stay with her until it was all over. The lady was only too happy to make me welcome and took me into her house. There were two little girls (four and seven years old), and they stood there wide-eyed, looking me over. I really did not feel comfortable there, but it was a temporary escape for me, and I was happy to stay. Outside, the temperature was something like 25 degrees below zero—it was one of the coldest winters that we had had for a very long time. Mama later told me that the men had a terrible time digging Papa's grave through the solidly frozen earth. It took five men several hours to dig it.

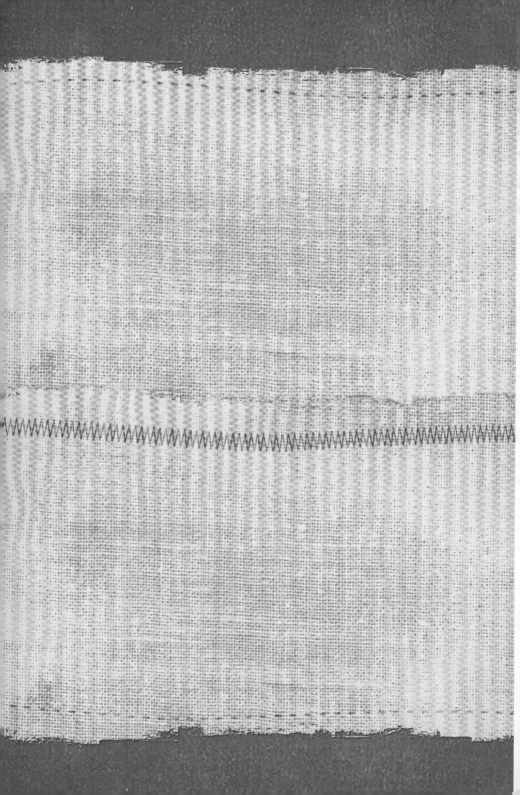

CHAPTER 29

LIFE WITHOUT PAPA

Mama and I stayed in the house (just the two of us), and we slept in the kitchen on the double bed where Papa had spent those bad times before he died. The rest of the house was big, and the rooms had high ceilings and big windows so it was impossible to keep such a big place warm enough to survive. The stove in the kitchen was joined through the wall to the chimney of the fireplace in the living room. The fireplace had a damper that we could close off and, therefore, keep the heat from the kitchen stove inside the kitchen. The kitchen was the perfect size to keep us comfortably warm, as long as we could keep a fire going in the stove.

Grandmother decided to return to the Great House even though it had been heavily damaged in the bombing. She did not want to leave her home empty, for fear that it would be bur-glarized or that the German soldiers would take it over. Mama and I were trying to make a life for ourselves, and we felt that it was safer in the village than it would be in Konstantinowka, where there was a lot of heavy fighting going on between the Russians and the Germans. The sounds of the cannons and the artillery could be heard, especially at night.

We were hoping to hold out until spring would arrive, but the cold winter was still to last at least three to four months. Occa-sionally we would make trips to the village to look for some food (mostly potatoes and carrots). We had made quite a few friends in the village. Mama had brought her sewing machine and some material (sheets, blankets, or any kind of material that would make clothing) from Grandmother's house. Mama would spend much time sewing (making) clothes, and from time to time, we took some things to the village where the people were happy to trade the clothing for whatever food they could give us. Some-times, we would spend all day long at the village, going from house to house bartering the clothes for food. We had to spend the night there on a few occasions, and some people would offer us a place to stay overnight. On most occasions, we would sleep in the stables, where there was a lot of straw to keep us warm.

It seemed that the people in the village tried to help us any way they could. A lot of the older people knew the Ljaschov fam-ily ever since the time when Grandfather owned the village. Some of the older men talked very favorably of our "old" family. Many of the village people had evacuated by train when the Russian troops pulled out. Those that stayed were bombed occasionally—and we never knew if the planes were Russian or German.

We were hoping that by the end of December, the very

cold weather would let up some and give us a break. In the meantime, we gathered wood outside by tearing down fences and breaking off branches of small trees. It was a daily chore to go around and pick up any wood that we could find to take home to make more fire. It seemed that we had nothing left on the outside to provide us with wood. So out of desperation, we started to burn chairs or whatever furniture we could do without. In the meantime, the temperatures outside were dropping to 42 and 54 degrees below zero, and we were quite desperate. The windows and the walls inside the house were covered with thick layers of ice (one and a half to two inches thick). We began to stay dressed with our coats, boots, and caps. We would sleep on the springs and put the mattress on top of us, then cover up with all the blankets, rugs, or anything else that would protect us from these terrible freezing temperatures.

By the time January arrived, the Germans began to fill any space that was available to live in. They would simply walk into the house and tell us that they needed a place to stay. When they arrived, most of them were sick, hungry, and half-frozen. They moved into the rest of our place, and they took all the beds and spaces until the house was full. We could no longer cook anything (mostly potatoes and carrots) without them coming into the kitchen and taking everything away—as soon as they smelled food, they would come and confiscate it.

JANUARY, 1942 • The Germans had overrun Belorussia (Belarus) and most of the Ukraine—Nonna's homeland. They had surrounded Leningrad (St. Petersburg) and had begun to converge on Moscow.

Soon Mama and I had only my small bedroom to ourselves—leaving the rest of the house to the German soldiers. They were coming in half-frozen and starved, and they were eating all our food supplies—which were already scarce. Soon they started to burn our furniture so they could sit by the fireplace and keep warm. Some of the soldiers were brought in on stretchers, and as soon as they could warm up, their ears and noses would drop off because they were frostbitten (actually frozen off). I watched one of the soldiers as he took his boots off by the fireplace: he had also taken off the skin of his feet all the way to the bone.

GERMAN SOLDIERS' SUFFERING • Hitler's soldiers suffered from the extreme cold climate of Soviet winters. They had not been equipped to withstand the freezing temperatures. Many German soldiers died in the winter of 1941 from cold exposure and frostbite.

Nonna reports on the troops at her house of refuge: "We end up with at least fifty-four German soldiers in our house, and they remain for a long time before the army trucks come and take them to a newly established German hospital."

Many nights, I lay in my bed awake, and I could hear Mama softly crying in her bed. She did not think I was awake and could hear her. Some nights, I would lay there and wish that my brother, Anatoly, would be there with us. I would imagine that by some miracle, he would just appear at our door. Even though I knew that it would never happen, I pretended that it could happen one day. Sometimes, I would feel angry because he was someplace else and knew nothing about what was happening with us. But then the thought of him being there—and the Germans killing him—would terrify me. He, too, could be killed or beaten to death like they had done to Papa and so many others. There were many very young boys along with men who were either tortured or beaten to death in these times.

Then I would be glad that he was someplace away, and I

would feel ashamed of myself for even wanting him to be with us. (What thoughts could go through the mind of a fourteen-year-old girl who was faced with the horrors that were all around us and from which there was no escape!) The only thing I was comforted with is what I had learned in my early childhood and what Papa had taught me: "Never give up hope, and look for the rainbows and happiness!"

Our next-door neighbor (who lived across the hall with her two little girls) and Mama decided that it would be better for us to move in with them into her kitchen and let the Germans have our place. There were five of us—Mama and me and the lady and her two small girls—and we felt a little more secure and a little warmer. Since there was no electricity or even candles to provide any light after dark, we would all settle down in a huddle around the table in the kitchen and tell stories or fairy tales for her children. Her girls were four and six years old, and we tried to make them feel safe.

We could hear the German soldiers across the hall singing and talking loudly. The lady we moved in with had saved some old, dry bread in small bags, and Mama and I would make trips to the nearby village to get some potatoes and carrots. So all of us shared what we had carefully—sparingly, eating just enough to keep us alive.

One day Mama and the lady (her name escapes me, but if my memory is correct, she called herself Marina, or Maria) decided to leave me and her two girls, with me in charge. They took a sack to go around the area and look for some wood for the fire in the stove, to give us some heat. Mama told me they would hurry and would be back home as soon as possible.

NEIGHBORS • Nonna's description of the housing arrangements is unclear. The village house appears to be laid out somewhat like a small apartment complex. Or, perhaps the woman lived across the street, rather than across the hall, whereas with the German soldiers in the house they could certainly hear them "across the hall."

Perhaps two or three hours passed since they had left. I was becoming worried when a few more hours passed and they were still gone. The little girls started to cry for their mother, and I tried every possible way to entertain both of them by telling stories and fairy tales. The sun went down, and it was getting colder outside. The fire in the stove began to die down, and the kitchen was getting colder.

I told the girls that our mothers would probably come home soon and that we should jump up and down, sing, or do whatever, to try to stay warm. So we started jumping up and down on the bed while holding hands and going around in circles. We kept reciting the Lord's Prayer—"Our Father which art in Heaven"— over and over again. I thought that we needed to pray, or sing, or do anything to pass the waiting time. Being still a child myself (fourteen years old), I wanted to cry badly, but I held on. I started to think that something really bad had happened to Mama and her friend. I began to think that I might be left with these little girls, and all kind of negative thoughts were going through my head. I tried to figure out how we would go through the oncoming night. Early in the morning I could take the girls to my grandmother's house—she surely would know what to do.

Finally, as I was having my worst thoughts, Mama and her friend stumbled against the door, and when I opened the door, what I saw scared me terribly. Mama and her friend stood there looking like two frozen mummies—they looked like they had been immersed in a pool of water that had frozen on them from head to toe. They were stiffened by solid ice, and they were shivering so hard that you could hear their teeth knocking.

There was a pot of water sitting on the stove, and it was still warm, so I dipped big towels into the warm water and wrapped Mama's and the lady's heads with the warm towels. Mama was moaning and grabbing her forehead and was saying that her head was very painful and she thought her nose and ears were frozen off. But they were not, and I assured Mama that everything was all OK. I took their frozen clothes off, wrapping Mama and Marina in dry blankets, sheets, and towels—just whatever I could find to make them warm. Mama cried with terrible pain in her back, and the lady, hugging her little girls, dropped off to sleep and did not wake up until daylight.

I wanted to know what happened to them, but I thought I would wait until Mama felt like talking. We broke a couple of chairs and made some more fire in the stove. I went outside to fill the big pot with snow so we could put it on the stove and make some more warm water.

The next morning, Mama told me what had happened. After they left home and walked around picking up scraps of wood here and there and putting it into their sack, German soldiers grabbed them and threw them into an old shack where there were some people already being held by the soldiers. The Germans were pouring water on them, and the water was freezing. This went on for a couple of hours, until some German officers came and freed them and told them to run home before they were frozen to the point of not being able to move. They were ordered to never be on the streets—ever again—for any reason! This was an act of those spiteful German soldiers thinking that they needed to pull a prank or an act of cruelty. However, I am sure that it probably caused some of the ones caught in that situation to get very sick, or maybe even die from colds or pneumonia. Mama continued to have headaches for a couple of weeks.

Eventually, we ran out of everything, and it was still a long time before spring would begin. Mama and I decided to move back to the Great House (or what was left of it) and stay with Grandmother. By this time, Grandmother had boarded up all the damaged parts of the house and stayed in one room, where she had installed a potbellied stove with a large flue pipe running through a hole in the window to let the smoke out—sort of serving as a chimney. On top of the stove, she could heat water and cook what little food she had. We went back to grinding the wheat kernels and making something resembling flour.

There was no cooking oil to cook with so Grandmother used (very sparingly) cod liver oil in the skillet to make pancakes. They tasted awfully fishy but were something to eat. We walked to the frozen fields and dug some frozen sugar beets (white). We would boil them for six to eight hours until they were edible—they were something else to eat. Grandmother tore half of her fence down to get more wood.

Needless to say, when spring finally did arrive, we got very busy planting anything that we could find to plant, and we felt that once again we had survived the worst!

CHAPTER 30

Surviving the German Occupation of Konstantinowka

Nonna recorded many miscellaneous childhood memories. These are a few, as well as two of her poems from that period.

I can feel my papa's gentle and loving touch and hear the words of his encouragement, the words of such wisdom. I feel his love and his gentleness.

• • •

I can smell the oil paint coming from the pavilion where Mama was painting.

• • •

I can hear Mama's singing and playing the piano or violin.

• • •

I can smell fragrances of flowers from my grandmother's gardens.

• • •

I can feel the breeze coming from the upstairs windows and see the swaying of those lace curtains . . . as a young child.

• • •

I can hear the laughter of my brother, Anatoly, and feel the strong grip of his hand—still a very young boy's hand.

• • •

FEELINGS

Today I had the sweetest feeling,

The world stood still for just a while.

I prayed to God as I was kneeling

And thanked Him for your sweetest smile.

FRIENDS

A good friend is like a glow in the darkness;

He brightens up your darkest thoughts.

When eyes are filled with tears, he harkens;

When you complain, he tires not.

It was sad to see the Great House in its damaged condition, and Grandmother living there alone. I remembered those beautiful years I had spent there when I was younger. With Petrovich not there, it did not seem like the same place, and of course, the damages from the bombings were pretty heavy. However, Grandmother was still the same warm, loving person that I remembered as a child. The nights in Konstantinowka were scary, since you could hear the German and the Russian artillery exchanging shots. The Germans were on the run, and they were hiding anyplace they could find. They were cold and hungry, many of them were injured, and some of them would die while in hiding.

Along in April and May, it seems that spring brought some quietness and peacefulness. Grandmother decided to make a big garden so we could plant some vegetables, and she planted some flowers next to the house. What she planted came in very handy. We ate from the garden and were careful not to waste anything. We consumed the tops and the bottoms of the vegetables. Of course, we did not have any meat, eggs, or milk, and we lived mostly on green stuff, but we did not suffer from hunger.

Since there was no electricity—not even candles or oil to burn the lamps—we would go to bed by dark—in the late afternoon or early evening. Grandmother and Mama would tell stories and reminisce, and we would try not to think about the days ahead since none of us knew what the future would bring for us.

Down at the railroads, there were still some trains moving, but no passengers were coming or going. I would run outside when I heard a train whistle blowing since I still lived with the hope that one day, somehow, Anatoly or someone else from my family would show up. Grandmother was hoping that Petrovich had somehow managed to get away and that he would appear. So, we lived mostly with a lot of hope, since it was giving us something to look forward to. But nothing happened, and we decided to make the best of the situation. People everywhere were like us—just kept going on and making the best of it. It took some more months for everyone to get used to it all. It was like we were in a state of limbo.

People organized a bazaar down on the outskirts of Konstantinowka and started selling or bartering for whatever anyone had. They were exchanging goods of all kinds, since money had no value. Mama and I were making regular trips to the bazaar, just browsing to see if there was some food or anything else that would be of value to us. We were happy to find anything that would help us survive those dreary times.

Mama and I decided to join the chorus at the Russian Orthodox church, and we went to practices for Sunday's singing at the church. I don't know where all the people came from for the Sunday services, but every Sunday, the church was packed. The services were typical of the Russian Orthodox Church, with all the candles, icons, etc., and I was looking forward to going there. Mama and I both sang very well, especially Mama, who sang in the first-soprano section. I sang mezzo-soprano.

I would get hungry, because the services were very long, and when the priest served the Lord's Supper, the little piece of bread was very welcome. It was just a small square of leavened bread, but it tasted so good, and the small taste of juice tasted good, also. Grandmother was extremely happy to be able to go to church again—she never missed a Sunday to be there. The evenings were long, and when the sunset would come, we prepared something to eat and once again retired to our beds before dark.

There were times when I was all to myself—engrossed in

my deep thoughts—and I kept a diary that I would hide in the old stable, under the carriage. There I would write about what it was like before the war, rather than what was happening now. I was hoping that if I kept writing about it, the old times would come back, and I could forget what was going on all around me.

• • •

A COLD MORNING • This particular memory, taken from the diary entry of December 1941/January 1942, appears in present-tense translation. It was written before Anna and Nonna moved back to the Great House with Grandmother.

It is a very cold morning—forty-two degrees below zero. As I look out the window I can see just a few hungry sparrows perched on the fence. The snow is about three feet deep. There is no wood anywhere to be gathered to build a fire to make our quarters warm in the big old house where we are living.

Papa was buried a few weeks ago, and Mama and I are trying to make our lives as bearable as possible. We know nothing about the future for both of us. Of course, at my young age, I am not worried so much about the future, and I mostly miss my dearest brother, Anatoly, and Papa. I lie in the bed by the window, and as I look out the window, there is a large, round moon looking right at me. It makes my heart just stand still. I lie this way—staring at the moon—and wonder why all of the things that are happening are happening. It does not seem right to be there without Papa and my brother and the rest of my family. Every once in a while, I can hear dogs barking or wolves howling near the long wooded stretch on the horizon. These kinds of sounds will stay with me for a lifetime. Sometimes the full moon gives off enough light to read and write by, and since there is no electricity or oil lamps, the light of the moon comes in handy. I can write in my diary, and I can think of a lot of things to put on paper. I eventually drift off to a gentle sleep.

At the crack of dawn, Mama and I plan for a new day and, of course, there is always hope that something will develop to change our way of living. Mama has cut up a few light blankets and made some children's clothes—coats, dresses, jackets, etc. Mama sits at the sewing machine and sews anything that comes to her mind.

This is a new day at sunrise—and what a beautiful sunrise it is—rising against a glittery frost. Mama and I are going to the village to trade the clothes she has made for food or things that we need. As we leave our house and I blow into the air, I see a diamondlike spray before my eyes, and the icicles cover my eyebrows and eyelashes. When we reach the village, we go to each door showing people our goods. Of course, we are paid with food such as bread, carrots, potatoes, meat, milk, etc. The villagers let Mama and me go into the stables and gather eggs or milk a cow for some milk. They seem so glad to see us with our goods, and they come from all over the village and offer us some food. The morning seems to have passed very fast, and as the afternoon approaches, the temperatures drop so cold that it is impossible to make the journey back home. Some of the villagers offer to let Mama and me spend the night by their huge fireplaces. They put blankets on the floor to make pallets for us to sleep on, and then we roast sunflower seeds over the open fire to snack on before we bed down for the night. It is so cozy lying here in front of the fireplace, and Mama and I soon drift off to a peaceful sleep.

The next morning, Mama and I make the journey back to our home. Mama is looking for more material from anything that we can do without, and she starts sewing again. There is not much to do after dark, and the darkness falls on us early—3:30 or 4:00 p.m., since the days are so short. The neighbors share light, and we have some old shoestrings and fish oil that we put into the lamp to make a little light. We sit around the small light and tell stories and wonder what is going to happen to us when the Germans move in. Little did we know the horrors and terrors that they would bring with them.

This is probably the coldest winter that we have ever had in this part of the Ukraine. Water is hard to find since everything is frozen solid, so Mama and I gather icicles and snow to melt over the fire to get water. The water that we drink has to be boiled for at least forty-five minutes. The Russians have moved out of our village, and they have destroyed much of what they left behind. The grain mills have been dynamited because the Russians destroyed anything that would be of use to the Germans—especially food.

The batters are about forty miles away from us, and the Germans are moving slowly due to the severe winter weather. Mama and I can hear the guns, cannons, and bombs and can see the light flashes from the battle in the distance. The horses are freezing to death and dropping on the roads. They are being cut up by the Germans (or whoever can get to them) and used as meat to survive. Mama and I stay away from all of this. We will not eat horse meat no matter how hard food is to find. I am still missing my horse, Sultan, which Grandmother gave to me for my eighth birthday. But out of the six horses that Grandmother had kept in her stables, there is only one horse left. The rest of them have been taken away by the Soviet government and have been shipped to the collective farms.

"BATTERS" • Probably Nonna meant *battle* here, or perhaps *batteries*. The transcript is unclear.

SULTAN • Nonna wrote about this particular horse: "I remember one of my grandmother's horses—it was a beautiful horse and so gentle. His name was Sultan, and he ate sugar cubes out of my hand. Grandmother wanted me to have him. But I just could not ride him. No matter how much Petrovich would try to get me on that horse, for some reason (unknown to me), I just could not do it. So I just called him my Sultan and visited him twice a day with some sugar cubes. I really loved Sultan, and I loved to brush his so shiny hair. And he stood so still while I brushed him. His eyes were so big, and his teeth were so white, and I think he was the best-looking horse in the stable."

All private farms have been made into collective farms, where the owners are forced to work there for the government. The cows suffer the same fate as the horses, and the one milk cow that Grandmother has left is taken away by the Russians before they pull out. We have to hide any warm clothing or food that we have left.

• • •

All my friends were gone except one or two girls that lived a few streets away (they were schoolmates). I stayed with Mama and Grandmother for fear that if I left the house and walked a few blocks away, something could happen to either one of us and we would not be able to find each other. Also the Russian planes flew over often and were shooting at people who were walking on the streets. Everyone was staying close to their homes. Many times I would sit on the steps and imagine that I was having a bad dream and that I would wake up and all would be just the way it used to be. I was a girl of many dreams, and I thought that I was reaching the age when I wanted to live my dreams out, but I had to comfort myself that there was a rainbow ahead—just like Papa had told me about.

There were plenty of German soldiers everywhere, and we

could hear them singing and playing accordions. They were staying in buildings that had been converted into barracks. However, we tried not to mix with them but rather stayed in our homes with the doors locked. We never knew what they would decide to do even though we never knew of any of them to bother us or to hurt us. The only time they would come close to us was when they were looking for food. Sometimes we would see them singing and marching down the streets, and we would go inside the house and watch them through the windows. Eventually some brave young girls would go down the street in an attempt to talk to them, but their commanders would chase the girls away. Occasionally you would see a German soldier talking to a woman, but the military police would see them and chase the girls away, and they would pick up any soldiers that tried to make friends with the Russian or Ukrainian girls. No one trusted anyone— the Germans did not trust us, and we did not trust them, so we isolated ourselves pretty well the whole time.

Eventually the Germans set up some organized offices and took full charge of policing. They opened some theaters where they were showing some movies, and even opened some grocery stores. They distributed some "quick money" (mostly in German marks), and since they needed some help, they were hiring our people. Some small communication was established with us, and the Germans began to act like they had already won the war —until they reached Stalingrad. There they met the strong push from the Russians, and all the "hell" of war broke loose, with the Russians pushing back with such force that it put the Germans on the run. They kept retreating, losing all their armies, and it was the bloodiest war all over again.

It was only a matter of time before they were moving out,

and there were no newspapers or other communications to tell us how close the retreating Germans were to us. We already knew that when the Russian troops came back, they would treat all of us as traitors because we had stayed behind and did not retreat with the Russians.

Mama and I had to find a way to leave and go west even if it meant traveling to Europe, so when the Germans offered us transportation to Germany, we had no choice but to take them up on the offer. The Germans needed some laborers in Germany's factories.

We heard later that those who stayed behind and did not leave Konstantinowka were thrown on trains and sent to Siberia or were killed. There really was no escape for us—one way or the other. Because Papa had always (for years) wanted to leave Communist Russia, we thought that we would go west. We did not see what was waiting for us in Hitler's Germany. We simply had to trust that we were making the right decision—and hope for survival.

Grandmother would sit by the fireplace with her hands folded in her lap (this was her favorite position) and say that she would keep the rest of the house intact until her family returned. She never stopped hoping, although Mama and I somehow knew that waiting for anyone to return was utterly hopeless.

STALINGRAD • Contrary to Nonna's account, it took months for the tide to turn in Russia's favor at the Battle of Stalingrad—Anna and Nonna had departed long before that. They might well have felt that "volunteering" to work in Germany was their only choice, but not because of retreating German soldiers or returning Russian ones. We can only speculate about her reasons for recalling the facts in this way; perhaps she attempted to rationalize what in retrospect must have seemed a horrible decision.

The Agony Continues

CHAPTER 31

AUGUST 1942

On August 7, 1942, Anna and Nonna said good-bye to Feodosija and boarded a train headed for a carton factory in Kassel, Germany. Packed into cattle cars with other women on their way to work in Germany, they traveled on the train for several days past Kiev, in the Ukraine, and on into Poland, Yevgeny's homeland. It was at one of the stops in Poland that the young Jewish woman tried to save her baby by tossing her into Anna's arms. Nonna's account resumes here, just after baby Sarah was discovered by the Germans and killed by one of the SS guards.

Everyone in our train car was in a state of shock. We were expecting the SS men to come back and investigate as to how the baby had been found inside our railcar. However, the SS men were preoccupied with other activity, huddled around the army trucks and talking to each other. Then our train started to move again, and it eased the tension somewhat. Once again, we all realized that we were prisoners of the Germans and were subject to the same kind of treatment they had given to little Sarah and her mother.

It was late in the afternoon, and the train picked up speed as we continued to cross Poland and head toward Germany. There was nothing but silence as night began to come. I suppose that we all were still in a state of shock. I know that Mama was—she was holding on to me very tightly. Eventually, I went to sleep out of pure exhaustion, and I slept most of the night. When I woke up the next morning, our train was still moving at a fast rate of speed, and the women on our car were very quiet and seemed to be in deep thought. It was as if none of them wanted to be the first one to say anything.

The train stopped again, and the SS men let us get off the train. Mama was thinking of finding a way to escape. She took me by the hand and walked away from the other people. I know that she was thinking about running away. But one of the SS men spotted us and shouted for us to come back. Mama found this little puddle of water and made out like she was washing her feet and my feet. Then we went back to the train because they were watching us very closely. We were loaded back on the train and continued to travel westward. We knew we were in Poland, but we had no idea as to what our location was—there was no way of knowing where we were.

I was thinking about little Sarah, and I was confused, angry, and sad about what the Germans had done. Also, I was trying to figure out what the Jews had done to be treated this way. There was no reason that I could think of, but I was to find out later about the atrocities and deaths that Hitler had planned for the Jews. Our train had slowed its speed somewhat, and the women had begun to talk about what we had witnessed and were a part of—yet everyone seemed to be in their own little world of thoughts and sadness. Our train had slowed its speed even more, and though we could not see anything, we felt that they were planning another stop. Little did we know that we were in for another shock that was as bad or even worse than what we had been through with little Sarah. It was beyond our comprehension that anything could be worse—but we were wrong.

"I WAS CONFUSED" • Here Nonna seems to have been grappling with anti-Semitism for perhaps the first time—another indication that she might somehow, amidst her own suffering, have been oblivious to the crisis.

Our train was approaching Lodz, Poland, and the train slowed. We continued to move at a slow pace until we came to a place where the Germans were "staging" railcars and sending the cars in different directions. The area was located out in a desolate spot where there were nothing but fields. As we approached, I could see some buildings that were situated near a large fenced-in area, with the fences being nine to twelve feet high. There was a double fence running through the center of this large fenced area. One side of the compound was where the Jews were being held, and on the other side the people from the East (Poles, Ukrainians, Russians, and others) were held for staging.

Our train had separated from a railcar loaded with Jews, and we were just sitting there, still hooked up to the locomotive engine. It was late in the afternoon, and the weather was cold and rainy. The Germans were very active—stirring around the area as if they were in a hurry to complete their mission. They had a lot of SS dogs alongside of them. There was a railroad track running into the fenced area where the Jews were held, and an adjacent track running into the area where the people from the East were being staged.

Our car sat there; we could hear the activity outside, and we knew that there were a lot of soldiers and SS men scurrying about. The dogs were barking, very excited with all the activity that was taking place. The Germans slid our railcar door open about eighteen inches or so and fed us a piece of bread, and they gave us some water in some kind of old rusty metal cups. The bread was dark in color, and it was just a chunk, as if the dough had been spooned onto a pan and baked. It certainly did not look good. As the Germans were feeding us, my attention was drawn to a railcar loaded with Jews. Their railcars did not have doors, but had iron bars across the door opening.

My attention was caught by a small boy who was standing inside the car, with his mother holding him by his thin little shoulders. He had his frail little arm sticking out through the bars and was making a begging motion with his little hand. As I looked at him, he was not much more than a skeleton, and his head seemed to be larger than normal. His eyes were deep set in his head and appeared to be very large. My attention was drawn to this little boy, and while I knew that there were a lot of things happening, I stared at this young boy and his skinny little hand begging.

I decided that I was going to give my bread to this young boy, but I needed to get out of our railcar and sneak over to where I could hand it to him through the bars of his car door.

I slid through the opening in our door and down to the ground. The Germans were very busy, and if they saw me, they didn't say anything. I ran over to the Jewish railcar and handed the chunk of bread to this young boy, who was murmuring something that was barely above a whisper. I knew that I had to hurry back and get into our car, but just as I turned around, the Germans were rushing toward the Jewish car along with their dogs, and they were shouting, "*Raus, raus!*"

As they unloaded the Jews from their car, I was caught up in this large group of people. A German soldier pushed me into the crowd and said, "If you want to feed them—join them!" The Germans were using large sticks and the dogs to herd this crowd of people toward a large field, and I was trapped in this rush of people and was being herded along with them. I was scared, and I kept looking back at the car where Mama and the other people were. However, the Germans continued to push, directing this large group of people toward that large field. As I looked back, I saw this little boy and his mother just a couple of feet away, and he was still clutching the chunk of bread in his little hand.

The German soldiers and the SS men were driving the crowd toward this open field where we could see a few Jewish men digging a large ditch. It started to rain, and everyone was running to keep ahead of the German soldiers and their dogs. Everyone seemed to know that we were going to be executed but did not dare to stop or try to escape. When we got to the ditch, the Germans made the crowd separate and line up in front of this large ditch that had been dug by the Jewish men. The little boy grabbed me and pulled me in front of him. His mother was clinging to his skinny little shoulders as they tried to stay together. The Germans started at the other end of the large ditch and made the men who had dug the ditch strip off all their clothing and stand there naked. All that I could think of was, "How did I end up here?" I was thinking of Mama back at the railcar, knowing that she was frantically looking for me.

Then the Germans began to shoot those poor people— one by one in the back of their heads, and they just toppled over into the ditch. They moved down the line of Jews, shooting them with their pistols—the shots sounded more like large firecrackers than guns. However, everyone knew what was coming—and as the Germans were three people away from this little boy and his mother and me, he grabbed me and gave me a heavy push into the ditch, which was now a muddy mess, a mix of mud and the blood of those who were being executed.

I landed facedown in this mess, with my head, face, and body covered in this bloody mud. It seemed like just a moment, but I heard this little boy's mother scream, "Nathan!" as the Germans shot both of them. Nathan's body landed on top of me and he did not move—his little body did not have much weight, so I lay there very still. I was afraid to move—even a little finger. I had turned my head so I could breathe before Nathan landed on top of me, and I lay there for what seemed to be an eternity before I opened my eyes after the shooting stopped and the German soldiers had moved away from the ditch.

When I opened my eyes, the first thing I saw was Nathan's body lying on top of me, still with the little piece of bread clutched in his little hand. I knew that Nathan and his mother were dead, and I was not sure if I was dead or alive. I could not feel any pain, but as I lay there, I realized that Nathan had saved my life by pushing me into the ditch just before the Germans shot. By doing this, he had saved my life before his frail little body fell on top of me and covered my body.

I continued to lie there for a long time, listening to every little noise. I could hear some talking not too far away; it sounded like a bunch of drunken men singing and cursing. It was dark, and I had heard about the reputation of the Germans to execute people just at dusk. However, with the rain and the heavy clouds, I could not tell what time it really was. I continued to lie there until I decided that I must get out of the ditch somehow and get back to Mama. I prayed that she was still there. I decided to move my fingers to see if there was anyone watching the ditch.

After a few minutes, all was still quiet, and I started to crawl to a place where I thought I could climb out of the ditch. But whenever I tried to climb up the ditch bank, I would slide backward into the blood and the mud. I continued to try to find a way out of the ditch—over and over again, I would slide backward. My face and body were covered with this heavy mud, and my head felt like a heavy ball. I finally found a spot where a small bush was hanging over the ditch. I grabbed a limb of the bush, but the limb was covered with sharp thorns. I broke the thorns off one by one until I could grab the limb and climb out of the ditch. I cleaned my eyes of the mud, but I heard some talking far away. I found a puddle of rainwater and tried to clean up as much as possible. I continued to hear the talking and decided to hide behind some bushes in case the Germans decided to return to the ditch.

By then it was nearing dawn—I could see the horizon begin to lighten up a little bit. When it became light enough, I started to walk to a wooded area near the field, thinking that it would be safer walking through the woods rather than across the field. I knew I had to walk back in the direction that the Germans had [taken] us. As I was walking through the woods,

I saw two German soldiers standing there talking to each other, and again, I didn't know whether to hide or to just keep walking. The soldiers saw me, and one of them came over and asked me what I was doing out in the woods at that time of the night, and I told him that I was lost from my mother and was trying to find her and get back to her. He told me to continue going toward the buildings way up ahead—he did not try to stop me, so I continued to walk in that direction.

When I got closer to the fenced area, I saw Mama standing by the fence looking toward me, but the next problem was for me to find a way to get inside the fence where Mama was. There were two SS men there. I was afraid that if they saw me they would shoot me or sic the dogs on me, so I decided to squat down by the fence and wait until I could slip through the gate. The SS men opened the gate to let the dogs out. Their attention was drawn away from my direction, and I slipped through the gate and ran to where Mama was standing. I know that Mama and I were in shock. She grabbed me and held me tightly. We sat there on the ground, cold and shaking—not a word was spoken between us.

CHAPTER 32

THE END OF THE LINE

When Mama and I got over the shock of my near-death experience, we fully realized that our lives were very much in danger. We would have to be extremely careful, and we would have to stay close to each other at all times. Finally, the Germans had put the train loaded with Eastern Europeans back together and continued the train on its way to Germany. We all knew that we were on the final leg of our journey from our homes and our families to work in the slave labor camps in Germany. The train was moving at a fast rate of speed, as if it were in a hurry to deliver us to our destiny in the labor camp.

When we reached the border between Poland and Germany, the train was stopped, and we were met by hundreds of Nazi SS men who were awaiting the train. The SS men ordered everyone to get off the train and to line up in columns of twos. They made us carry our luggage or whatever we had on the train, and Mama and I stayed together as the SS men started to march us across the border, where there were trucks loaded with barrels of soup.

Each of us was given a rusty-looking metal container that was filled with a brew that smelled like bad cabbage, with bits of carrots and maybe cabbage leaves in the soup. We were given a chunk of dark bread, and we were allowed to eat while sitting on the grass. After we had finished eating, the SS men ordered everyone back into the columns of twos, and we started marching.

Everyone was wondering where we would end up. After we marched for several hours, they let us stop and go into the bushes and then rest for a few minutes—then start marching again. This went on all afternoon, and my little feet were so very tired, and my legs felt like they were cramping up. All the women were so very tired and weak, but the Germans made us continue to move. My shoes were too small for me. Mama had cut out the toes of my shoes, but they were still uncomfortable.

At dusk, we reached a spot where the Germans told us that we would stop for the night and ordered everyone to gather in a huge group so they could guard us. We were all bone tired; we just huddled together in an attempt to stay warm, since it was the fall and the nights would get quite cold. I suppose that we all got some sleep by leaning against each other, and somehow we made it through the night. Early in the morning, before daybreak, we awoke to the sounds of motors from a bunch of trucks coming our way. We were loaded onto those trucks in groups until there was standing room only, and the trucks took off—each one loaded with as many people as it would hold.

Mama and I held on to each other so we would not get separated, because no one knew where they were taking us.

Soon we reached a place in a field that was fenced in with a tall fence, and there were a few buildings located inside. Once there, they made us all unload from the trucks, and they ordered us to line up our luggage or suitcases next to a fence inside the compound.

LUGGAGE • Because these women were headed to a labor camp—not an extermination camp (a killing center), like the Jewish passengers—they were allowed to keep their luggage. In her transcript, Nonna did not always make the important distinction between the types of camps.

We were kept there for about ten days while the Germans deloused everyone. They shaved many of the women's heads and made them shave under their arms and even their groin area. Then they came by with a bucket of liquid and painted this solution over our naked bodies with a paintbrush—then everyone was given a physical exam to check for any diseases.

The SS men were there with the dogs, guarding the barracks and the area inside and outside the fences. The barracks did not have any mattresses, and we were told that we were to sleep on a cot made out of boards. They told us not to leave the area of the barracks, and especially not to go near the tall outside fences, since these were electrically charged and we would be electrocuted if we touched them. They fed us soup and bread, but there was no work to be done, so we spent our days waiting for whatever was to come. We were all praying that we would not be sent to the concentration camps. They took away all our clothes and gave us a uniform made with stripes so that no one could possibly escape. The Germans gave everyone cloth badges to stitch on the outside of the uniforms. The people from Russia and the Ukraine were given badges that read *OST*, which means "east." The Polish people were given badges that had a large *P*, which stood for "Polish." They gave us a needle and thread and told us that the badges must be worn where they could be seen at all times.

So we waited for their next move and just spent our time thinking about what was in store for us. I was standing in the doorway of the barracks when my attention was drawn to a small boy who was reaching under the fence to pull up a rutabaga that was sticking up in the field outside the fence. This boy looked to be six or seven years old, but he was very thin, and even his neck was thin and long. I watched as he pulled the rutabaga under the fence, wiped the dirt off on his clothes, and took a bite out of it.

Just then, a Nazi soldier, who was fat and had a loud voice, came up and began to curse the little boy and called him a thief. The Nazi was carrying a large umbrella that had a curved handle, much like that of a walking cane, and the Nazi stuck out the curved handle and caught the little boy around his small neck with the handle. He began to swing the little boy around by his neck—first one way then the other way until the little boy's feet were off the ground. The soldier was laughing and cursing, and continued to swing the little boy around and around. I saw what was happening and wanted to run over there and stop the soldier, but after my narrow escape with Nathan, I was afraid to interfere. I probably could not have done much, anyway. There were two more German soldiers that came over and ordered the soldier to stop swinging the little boy, and when he stopped swinging him, the boy just dropped to the ground. When the other soldier picked his little body up, his head was just hanging loosely, and I knew that the soldier had killed the little boy by breaking his neck.

Once again, that sick feeling came over me; this was another incident that I must carry the memories of for all my life. By this time, we didn't know what to expect next. Every one of the prisoners was heartsick, but we were helpless to change anything. We were just hoping that we would not be the next victim.

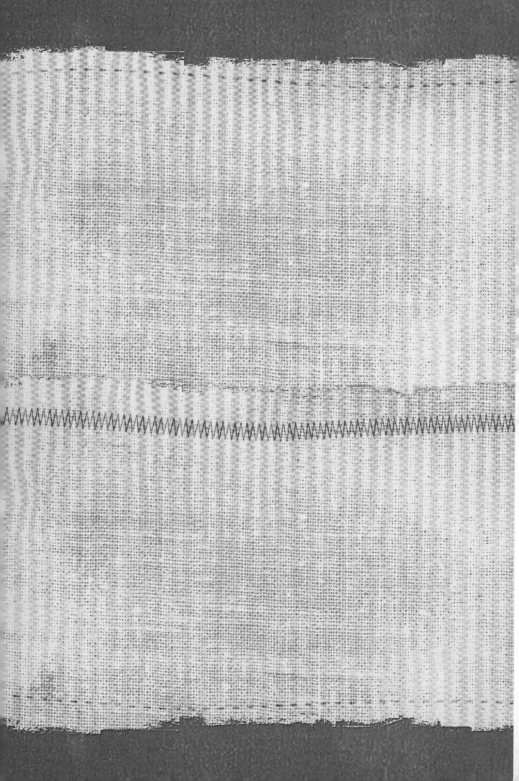

CHAPTER 33
IDENTIFICATION PATCHES

As soon as we arrived in the first labor camp in Kassel, Germany, we were given patches! We were given one dozen of the patches each, given out by nationality, with the Russians and Ukrainians getting the same patch—OST. We were also separated by nationality in the labor camps. The Jews were immediately put in the Yiddish camps, and the Russians and the Ukrainians were put together into East, or Russian, camps. The Jews were given patches that were in the design of the Star of David and had a blue outline with an orange center—with *Yiddish* in the center of the star. The Poles were issued a diamond-shaped patch that had a yellow center with the letter *P* in the center.

We were put behind bars in barracks that were surrounded by barbed-wire fences (some electrified) about nine to ten feet tall. The gates to the camps were guarded by SS men who had many dogs with them. There was no way possible to escape because we had to wear our patches, anyway. Every day we were marched to our places of work—some worked in factories, and some cleaned streets after the bombings. I guess the Poles had more privileges and choices than any of us. We were not allowed to be free on the streets, and of course, the stores were "off limits" to us and the Jews. Quite often, there were some prisoners who would dare to go into the stores without a patch, but when the SS caught them, the punishment was severe—being shipped to the concentration camps.

The Poles invented a kind of "black market" by trying to exchange or offer us their "P" patches—sometimes for money (but there was really no one who had money). However, they would barter for things like an umbrella or whatever we had to give up. If a prisoner had some extra bread or cheese, she might exchange it for the "P" patch. This practice lasted but a short time, because if a Jew would accept a Polish "P" patch so she could find a better place to hide from the SS men, she would be shot and killed. Sometimes, a Pole would tell the SS men that some Jew had accepted a "P" patch for a piece of jewelry or something. The SS men would take the Pole and the Jew into the field and shoot them both. The Poles soon stopped this practice after seeing what the consequences were.

No one could trust anyone! We would hang around, work, and be locked up in the camps. We were fed a rusty can of cabbage soup and a three-by-three-inch piece of bread daily. Sometimes they would take us for a walk (exercise, I guess). In the camps, people did not talk much for the first three to five months because no one knew who was a friend and who was an enemy.

Mama and I were glad that we had each other so we could talk and keep each other company.

• • •

October 1942

I no longer know what the future holds for us—for me. I know that I am no longer a child, but also not yet a woman.

Now I can only imagine what could be—but is not. I am not free, and yet not held imprisoned.

• • •

November 1942

The snow is piling up high—it looks for a moment as though we are back home—our beautiful "palace," as I called it. Perhaps I am asleep and will awaken soon. It could be only a bad dream—I hope.

CHAPTER 34

LABOR CAMP, OUR FIRST ASSIGNMENT

1942

Finally the SS men told us that a group of us were being transferred to a factory in Kassel, Germany. They had all of the prisoners assemble, and they called out the names of those being transferred—Mama and I were included in the first group.

They loaded us onto trucks and took us to an *Arbeitslager,* a labor camp, in Kassel that supplied workers for a *Kartonfabrik* (carton factory). We were assigned to barracks in a large building inside a fenced-in compound, and everyone was relieved to see that we would have a bunk to sleep on. They were three-tiered bunks but were really an improvement from what we had been accustomed to! The work in the factory was not really bad; our job was to spread glue on the cartons after the machinery formed them. Mama and I had begun to have some hope that we could survive and that, when the war was over, we could make a life for ourselves.

The worst times were when we were not working—we were locked up and had nothing to do to pass the time. There were no books to read and no games (chess or checkers) to play—not even playing cards to take our mind off of our plight. I remember that Mama brought some scraps of cardboard from the factory, and she made a deck of cards with pencils and colored pencils that the man who was in charge of our camp had supplied her with. We would play simple games of cards. Mama continued to make these decks of cards until we had more than one deck to play with and the other prisoners had a chance to join in on the card games. Mama even drew kings, queens, jacks, etc., with the colored pencils, and everyone really appreciated her ingenuity and talent. During this time, we began to talk to each other more, and we began to make some friends. This helped to pass the time while we were locked up and not working at the factory. Everyone joined in sharing with others, and there was some hope that things would improve with time.

The time was getting close to Christmas, but there was no snow such as we had been used to in Russia, Ukraine, and Poland. The sun was very bright, but it was cold in Kassel at this time of the year (December). Mama was painting a picture for the Kommandant of our labor camp. He was a short, stocky civilian who, along with his family, lived in a big apartment building next to our camp. He would bring some postcard pictures and some oil paint and canvas so Mama could paint them to a larger size, and he would hang them in his apartment. We all benefited from Mama's art talent and the beautiful work that she produced. The Kommandant would bring us some special treats occasionally——such as onions, carrots, and oatmeal cookies. We would line up, and the lucky ones would catch something as he came into our huge room (which housed eighty to eighty-five of us prisoners). We would share the goodies with those who did not catch anything.

The windows of our barracks were barred with heavy metal bars, and as you looked out the windows, all you could see was the big red-brick wall of the apartment where some of the Germans lived. Sometimes you could hear the voices of some German children playing, and they would yell at us and make fun of us by calling us "jailbirds" and other names.

GERMAN CHILDREN • These were children of the German officers who ran the camps. German children had many advantages over the children in the cold barracks—food, clothing, playgrounds. Some camps even built zoos for the German officials' children.

We were marched from the camp every morning at 5:00 a.m. to the factory, which was about two miles away, always guarded by the SS men and their dogs. Then they would watch us while we worked at the tables putting glue on the paper and making different sizes of cartons. Every day, they would count how many cartons each person made (like it was a contest). Those who made the biggest pile of cartons were awarded with an extra bowl of cabbage soup or an extra piece of bread. Therefore, we all worked our fingers and hands as fast as we could. We would exchange greetings as we came into work by saying "Heil Hitler" to anyone that we passed by, following the custom obediently because we knew that we were being watched closely. This custom was like worshiping the Führer as God, and if we didn't say

"Heil Hitler," we were punished by not getting any food for that day—so we all followed this custom very closely.

HITLER SALUTE • Eastern laborers were required to respectfully greet the Germans, but the actual salute was required of only the Germans themselves.

• • •

December 1942

We are always looking out the windows through bars—why these bars when no one can go anywhere through the locked gates?

The dogs are watching—the soldiers are walking restlessly, and they look so cold! Wonder if they wish they could trade places with us who are behind these barred windows. What do they really believe in? Do they really think that *Hitler* can conquer this world? It will never happen!

It is almost Christmas—my thoughts are wandering back to the Christmas of 1932, which I spent at Grandmother's Great House in the village. I remember the sleigh ride with all of us piled up in the sleigh. I am fifteen years old—has it really been ten years since that beautiful time?

I really miss Grandmother. Wonder what happened to her when the Russians came back. Who lives in our beautiful house? Who picks the fruit from our orchards?

• • •

When December 24 came, which happened to be Mama's birthday, everyone wanted to celebrate Christmas. Mama had just finished one of Herr Schuller's paintings, and it was still wet when she rang the bell for him to come and get it. We told him that we wanted him to have it as a Christmas gift, and he was quite touched when he saw that beautiful painting.

HERR SCHULLER • Presumably, Nonna refers to the Kommandant here.

He came back with a big bag of large tea cookies that his wife had baked. He gave everyone a cookie, and we were all touched by his generosity. We asked him to find us a small branch (there was no hope for a real pine tree). He found us a small branch that did resemble a tree, and it smelled like pine. He also brought us some colored construction paper and some glue, and we all sat around making a chain out of paper. We also cut out some snowflakes and made an angel to put on top of the "tree." We hung some pieces of cookies from the tree—then, in several languages (Polish, Russian, Ukrainian, and some others, like Latvian), we sang some carols. There was a little Christmas in each of us, but our celebrations didn't last long before the German guards pounded on our locked door and yelled for us to be quiet. We were happy that we did get to celebrate the Baby Jesus' birthday—however short the party had lasted. After Christmas, we were ready to march back to the factory, and none of us knew what the next day would bring!

• • •

January 1943
What do other people think of people like Mama and me? How did the German generals find out that Mama can paint? She is painting away all day long—what will

they do with all her paintings later? (Maybe they will sell them to the British or Americans.)

• • •

We were relatively comfortable; the Germans were feeding us our ration of soup and bread, and the work was not too difficult. However, the barracks were not well heated, so Mama and I slept together on one cot so we could double the cover and try to stay warm. There were German workers at the same factory. We were kept separated from them by a heavy metal fence— but we could see them and speak to them through the fence. Gradually, we were able to make some friends, and they would occasionally sneak us a cookie or some other kind of food.

We worked at this factory for about six months without any incidents, until one day a couple of SS men came to our barracks area and went in and talked to our Control Officer for about an hour. Then they came to our area and asked, "How many of you are Russian?" We raised our hands. Then he asked, "How many of you are Ukrainian?" We raised our hands. Then he asked, "Is there anyone here that can speak fluent German?" I was hesitant to raise my hand because Mama could not speak German, and I didn't want to be separated from her.

When he asked the question again, I raised my hand and told him (in German) that I could speak German. He looked at me and said, "Then talk to me in German—I will talk to you, and you answer me in German." After several sentences, he asked me where I had learned to speak the German language so well. I was afraid to tell him that I had learned it from Papa, so I told him that I had just "picked it up," since I had an interest in languages. He told me that he needed me at another factory where there were people of several languages working. I told him that Mama was here and I didn't want to leave her. He asked, "Where is your mother?" I pointed to Mama, who was sitting on a bench. He called Mama to come join us, and he told us that we were being transferred to a *Textilfabrik* in Lichtenau, Germany, which was about a hundred and fifty miles away. He and a younger SS man took us in a car and we left for our new assignment.

On the way, we had a conversation about how many languages I could speak, and he asked if I could speak the Jewish language. I told him that I could not speak Yiddish but that I could understand and translate the language. It took us several hours to reach the new labor camp. He kept assuring us that we were not being taken to a concentration camp but that we would be assigned new duties at the textile factory. When we arrived, he took us into the factory. The noise was so loud that we could not hear anything. He showed us the machinery and asked if I thought that I could do this work. I assured him that I could and that Mama would be an expert. He asked to look at my hands and kind of shrugged at my small young hands. Then he and the younger SS man left, and we never saw them again.

We were assigned to the prison barracks, which were about six miles from the factory, and we were again surrounded by barbed-wire fences. Our living conditions were about the same, but the food was a little better there, and each barracks building had a potbellied stove that kept us warm at night. We had to march to work and from work—this meant that we had to get up at about 4:00 a.m. and march to work guarded by one SS man and one dog for each twelve of the workers. However, we were not mistreated, and we gained the trust of our camp

Kommandant, who took a liking to Mama and me. He knew that Mama was an artist and could paint some beautiful art, so he would bring her oil paint and canvas and ask her to paint pictures for him and his wife. Our workload lightened, and soon they were letting us go on breaks to a wooded area where there were pine trees—we felt privileged to get this opportunity. There was no way to get away because of our clothing and the badges—everyone knew that we were "labor camp" people.

After a few months of working at the Textilfabrik, the Germans moved us to another compound near the trees and told us that there was no more work for us [. . .]

"NO MORE WORK FOR US" • The transcript breaks off here, apparently missing a page. Anna and Nonna were taken to a porcelain factory at Buchenwald, Germany, near Weimar, in the hills of Germany. There, Nonna came down with tonsillitis and ran a high fever.

[. . .] of tonsillitis and was running a pretty high fever. The camp Kommandant brought me some aspirin to help with the fever—aspirin was about the only medicine that was available. While we were in this camp, we considered ourselves very lucky except when one of us would get sick and we had to take care of ourselves. I remember one of the girls started to run a high fever, and we called the Kommandant and told him that this girl was very sick. He came and brought some aspirin, but when her fever caused her to lapse into unconsciousness, he decided that he had better call the doctor to make sure that it was not contagious. As it happened, she had developed scarlet fever, and they came and moved her out. We didn't know where they took her, but they disinfected the whole area in the camp and took her bed and all her belongings away. We never knew what happened to her, but we kept quiet when we would get sick!

We were OK as long as we could march to the factory and work. I had developed a very badly infected toe (caused by shoes that were too short). I started to limp because the pain was getting unbearable. The Kommandant noticed me limping, and he brought me some medicine and told Mama to cut a hole in the shoe over the infected toe, which had already begun to turn black. The Kommandant brought a pair of pliers and pulled the toenail out, and I got relief immediately. I was happy that the infection did not spread.

We all tried to doctor our own illnesses, and we helped each other the best we knew how, since we didn't know what had happened to our friend. It was some time later that we were told that the sick ones were being gassed or burned in the concentration-camp facilities. We thought it was only rumor, but we could believe that this was happening and we no longer took any chances by complaining!

Several weeks passed, and again we were visited by the SS men. They went in and talked to the camp Kommandant for a while, and he came out and told Mama and me to pack our things because we were being transferred back to the factory in Kassel.

By that time, my German was fluent, and I had picked up a few more languages from other prisoners at the textile factory. Once again, we were taken by car on the long ride to Kassel, but on this trip, there was no conversation taking place.

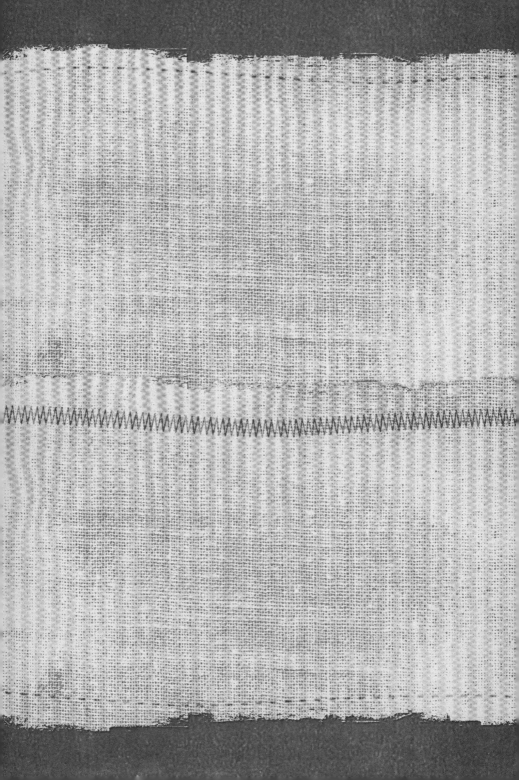

CHAPTER 35

THE BREAK
Spring 1943

February 1943

We are moving out today—I think they want Mama and
me in a better place. But would this mean more freedom
for us? They listen to me speaking, and they look so
stupid to me. Is it so unusual for anyone to speak more
than two languages? They are so dumb! Papa was wrong
about them and their intelligence. These people are not
even smart—they are just greedy, I think. Maybe even
here there are some good people. Where are they?

• • •

Soon after we were returned to Kassel, Mama and I got a real
good break—the Germans transferred us to work in a hospital

that had been built for the prisoners of war and people from the labor camps.

HOSPITAL WORK • This move proved most fortunate for Anna and Nonna. Yevgeny had been right to forearm Nonna with the ability to speak fluent German and other languages.

This hospital was for all nationalities. It was built like barracks and was adjacent to the Catholic hospital at Marienkranken-haus, Germany. When we arrived at the hospital, two Catholic nuns came out to greet us and were joined by the priest. They were so friendly and so kind that Mama and I were a little bit in awe! The nuns directed us up to the fifth floor of the Catholic hospital and assigned a room for us to live in. The room was very pretty and clean with two nice beds in it—Mama and I just couldn't believe that we could be so lucky and that we would not be forced to live in the barracks of a labor camp surrounded by barbed wire! The nuns also told us that we could take our meals there in the hospital—Mama and I were so happy. At last our ray of sunshine had come through. We decided that we would give them our best effort in our work to make up for their kindness.

"RAY OF SUNSHINE" • The Catholic hospital must have seemed like paradise to Nonna and Anna. They had been sleeping on mattressless boards at the camps, and here they had real, clean beds. They also enjoyed good healthy food instead of stale bread and watery, rusty cabbage soup. Though they were still technically prisoners, the nuns and priests treated them like valued coworkers.

The hospital was run by a Catholic order, staffed with nuns and priests, and was considered to be one of the better hospitals in Germany. The French prisoners of war had built a bunker in the rear of the main hospital, to be used during the war. The bunker was four floors underground and had two floors aboveground. There were no elevators in the bunker, so everyone was forced to use the stairwells to move from floor to floor—this was quite inconvenient when we had to move patients around.

Mama assumed her duties of working the regular wards of the prisoners' hospital, which was built behind the bunker area, and was able to return to the main hospital when she was off duty. I started my duties in the admitting office of the prisoners' hospital and was taught to type on an old manual typewriter by Sister Pia, who had taken a liking to me.

I was young and eager to learn anything to come my way, but the main thing that I was doing was translating and helping with communications between the nurses and the patients. There were all nationalities of people who had been taken prisoner and were being held in regular prison camps, but when they would get sick, they would be sent to this hospital for treatment. There were even some American soldiers that came to the hospital for treatment, but at that time, I was not fluent in the English language. Mama and I were very happy that such good luck had come our way, and we were treated like family members by the priests and nuns.

• • •

Spring 1943
I like this place called Marienkrankenhaus. The nuns are very kind, and I like the job of interpreting for Dr. Hoffman. He is a good man. I would not mind to be a doctor and work in the operating rooms. I wonder if this would be all right with Papa—me in the medical profession. Maybe I will become a nurse.

Schwester Pia is teaching me to work in the admitting

office and to type. I like her a lot—she is so patient with me. So are Sister (Schwester) Longa and Sister Mauricia.

Today I spent some time with Sister Mauricia in the lab. Every night now, I will be studying in the library. They gave me a test today, and Herr Dr. Hoffman (I like him) thinks that I am ready to finish my high school education soon—I think so too. What I have learned is elementary "junk." It is good enough for Lena—not for me, though.

LENA • Here she probably refers to herself as "Lena." The nuns gave Nonna the German name Lena Schulz to hide her identity.

• • •

Some of the doctors, including the chief of staff at the prisoners' hospital, were old emigrants from Russia and Poland. Even though Mama did not speak German, she was able to communicate with these doctors since she spoke and understood both Russian and Polish, and she seemed to be very happy. However, one of the old Russian doctors began to make advances toward Mama. She tried everything to discourage him. He was much older than Mama, who was then thirty-seven years old and a beautiful woman. His name was Dr. Schevchenko. He was persistent in his pursuit of Mama, and he would follow her around trying to grab her—he even asked Mama to have an affair with him. This was the last thing that Mama was thinking about under the circumstances we were in.

One day he was walking behind Mama, making fresh remarks, and tried to grab her rear; when he did, Mama turned around and slapped him very hard. Of course, he got very mad and really talked ugly to Mama, then stormed off. One of the other doctors told Mama that Dr. Schevchenko was really mad at her; he told Mama to stay away from him—that he could cause a lot of problems for her. This worried Mama, but she was a high-spirited woman, and in some ways she was daring in some of the things she did.

I told Schwester Blonda the story about old Dr. Schevchenko and his advances to Mama and said that Mama did not want to get involved with him. I also told her what the other doctor had warned Mama about. The *Oberschwester* (Mother Superior), Sister Blonda, told Mama that she was going to move her from the prisoners' hospital to the main German hospital to get her away from Dr. Schevchenko. Mama was transferred to work in the main hospital in the contagious ward where people with communicable diseases were treated. I continued to work in the admitting office of the prisoners' hospital, and I also spent some time working in the admitting office of the German hospital. Mama and I continued to live in our room on the fifth floor, but we were worried about what had taken place. Also, the nuns began to worry about Mama bringing some communicable disease germs and exposing me, so they decided to move Mama to regular duties in the main hospital.

"THE NUNS BEGAN TO WORRY" • The nuns apparently didn't worry about Anna's contracting germs herself from the communicable disease ward, but they were concerned for Nonna's sake. Perhaps this was because of her weakened state or, possibly, their regard for Nonna's language ability and services.

The nuns were like angels sent from heaven to save Mama and me from the terrible things that we had been through. We were happy, yet there was always the cloud of uncertainty (maybe even fear) that seemed to occupy our thoughts. Mama always tried to keep a smile and reassure me that we would be all right, that the war would soon be over and she and I could make a life of our own and fulfill some of the dreams that Papa had shared with us. However, we felt a great deal of security with the Catholic nuns and priests taking care of us and shielding us from the unrelenting terror that the Nazis had unleashed against so many innocent people.

"ANGELS SENT FROM HEAVEN" • Nonna believed that the Catholic nuns at Marienkrankenhaus actually saved her life. She later credited them with hiding her from her enemies and protecting her from danger.

Nonna doesn't specifically acknowledge the generous amount of freedom she and Mama had at Marienkrankenhaus—even though they were prisoners there. But a photograph of Kaiser Wilhelm's *Schloss* (castle) in Kassel, Germany, and its caption show that the two women must have enjoyed free time through the kindness of the nuns, even though they were officially incarcerated at the Catholic hospital by the Nazi government. The caption reads, "Kaiser Wilhelm's Schloss. Mama and I visited frequently while we were employed in Marienkrankenhaus."

A second photograph shows part of the castle grounds: a peaceful valley, graced by a white gazebo and a small pond. Beneath that photograph Nonna wrote, "My little gazebo! This is where I would go and spend many hours reading books, writing in my diary, and just think! This was located behind the castle (seen in the background). I would watch the swans swim on the lake."

June 1943

Tomorrow is Dr. Hoffman's wedding. He and Hilga are finally getting married. (Perhaps I should have been born ten years sooner!) Just one of my stupid thoughts! I really like them both very much. Hilga has been a good friend to me, and I have learned so much from Dr.

Hoffman—even stitching wounds. The wedding will take place in the chapel of the hospital. (How sad that it has to be celebrated in such a small way.) Mama will play the organ, and Dr. Ingrid Nubel will sing. Father Antonius will do "his thing"—he is so fat and funny! I wonder: if Hilga has children, what will they look like? Dr. Hoffman is so tall and has black hair, and Hilga is so short and has flaming red hair. If they have a baby girl, she may look tall and have red hair. I hope that I don't think about it during the ceremony. I might laugh and get into trouble with the ushers!

Wedding Day: *Liebes Gott!* I hate this dress Sister Blonda wants me to wear—it is ugly and stiff. The only good thing is that it is blue. Maybe I will hide behind Sister Maria (ha ha) when they take pictures. I'll be glad to get out of this dress. Why do they all want me to look like them—when I am not? They (the sisters) won't let me wear my hair down, tied with a bow—these braids, how I hate them! I look like a German maiden who just came from Sudetenland and am waiting to become a nun (ha ha)—I might just as well laugh about it all. If I ever get out of this place, I will cut my hair short. Hope it is soon. Well, I am really happy for Hilga and Dr. Hoffman and will miss them for the next two weeks.

CHAPTER 36

LOSS OF MAMA
September 1943

It was early in September, and my most important birthday was approaching—"Sweet Sixteen." I was very excited and was cautiously thinking about the life that was ahead of us. Mama and I had made plans to celebrate my birthday—she was going to arrange for a birthday cake, and we were going to have a party with our friends at the hospital.

When I woke up on the morning of my birthday (September 22), Mama was already getting ready and told me that she had to make a little trip. I was unaware that the Gestapo had sent her a letter telling her to report to the Gestapo headquarters for some document verification. I was upset because Mama and I had made plans to spend some time together on my birthday, and then there was the party that we had planned.

I begged Mama not to go on my birthday, to wait until the next day to make the trip. However, she explained to me that this matter could not be put off.

We met briefly at breakfast time and spoke again before we said our good-byes at the hospital entrance. We were both in a cheerful mood. She had promised that she would return in a couple of hours, and then we would celebrate my birthday.

After six or seven hours, I was concerned because Mama had not returned, and I didn't know what had happened to her. In desperation, I went to the Oberschwester and begged her to call the place where Mama went to find out if she was still there. However, she (Schwester Blonda) was very hesitant to make that phone call for me—for the first time I was told that the place where Mama had to appear was the headquarters of the Gestapo in Kassel to report for document verification. Mama had not told me where she was going to keep me from worrying.

A feeling of terror struck me then, since I had heard stories about how the Gestapo operated. I had been told how people would go there, and no one would ever see them again. It usually happened to the Jews, and I was quite confused at that time as to what reason they would even have to call my mama.

The Mother Superior (Schwester Blonda) very reluctantly made one phone call to the Gestapo headquarters and asked about my mother. They gave no explanations, and when she tried to ask questions, she was told to never call that number again and they hung up. Schwester Blonda was somewhat terrified, and she told me that it was not safe, or even a good idea, to try to reason with the Gestapo, and she told me that we would just have to wait and see if Mama would return. It was two or three days later when the Mother Superior told me that the Gestapo had made a written request for them to turn me over to them voluntarily. Thinking that I would see my mama there, I was only happy to report to the Gestapo.

I was escorted by one of the hospital's employees, and we got on the streetcar and headed toward the Gestapo building. I could see fear in my companion's eyes as we entered the door to the building, but I could not fear anything that I was not fully aware of. I was only sixteen years old, but since I was so small and thin, many people thought I was only ten or eleven years old. There were times when I had to use my intelligence and cleverness to escape—yes, even tell a lie.

Two uniformed SS men came out and led me into a large room where there was one desk sitting in the middle of the room. There was a picture of Hitler on the wall, and next to the portrait, there was a flag with a huge swastika on it. There I stood in front of the desk looking at the SS man sitting behind the desk, and I was wondering what was going to happen next. For perhaps five or six minutes, the SS man stared at me with those bottomless gray eyes, and it was difficult to read any kind of expression in them. It was almost as though his eyes were looking through my whole little body without meeting my eyes. If I live to be a hundred years old, I could never erase the feeling that his stare gave me.

I started to tremble, not with fear but from being uncomfortable. He never said one word, and I decided that I had to say something first. The first thing that entered my mind was Mama, and before I realized it, I was saying, "What have you done with my mother?"

As I spoke these words, the SS man who was standing by

the door approached me and hit me on the side of my head with the butt of his pistol. He then pressed the barrel of the pistol against my head, and it felt so very cold. He said, "So you are Russian. Maybe you would like to play Russian roulette?"

Suddenly I realized what was happening to me and the danger that I was in, but for some unknown reason, I didn't panic, and suddenly I no longer cared what would happen to me. So I smiled right into the eyes of the SS man who was sitting behind the desk. He shrugged as though he was surprised at my bravery, and he ordered the SS man (who looked no older than twenty-two or twenty-three years old) to put his pistol away and get back to the door, severely reprimanding the young SS man for his actions.

Then he began to ask me some questions. The first question was, "How old are you?"

At this time, I knew that somehow he knew my real age and only wanted to hear what my answer would be and perhaps catch me in a lie. So, looking him straight in the eyes, I told him the truth, which was that my birth certificate was changed prior to deportation from the Ukraine so that Mama and I could travel to Germany together and would not be separated.

I guess my answer surprised him, and he gave me a long, searching look, saying, "Why do you think that telling the truth now would make a difference for you? It's already too late for your mother. I could not possibly arrange for her return. Besides, her birth certificate was not the only reason that she was shipped out."

This was precisely how he put it, and then he proceeded with more questions. When he came to the story of how Mama had tried to save the baby Jewish girl, he demanded that I tell him how it really happened, since he already knew the facts from the other witnesses that were there. The only thing I could tell him was the truth, that neither my mother nor I knew that the baby was Jewish and that Mama was still in mourning from losing her own baby, that it was purely an emotional act to grab the baby and try to save it.

I was almost shocked as he listened to my story because for a brief moment he looked as if there was a flicker of compassion in his eyes. Then he said, "Very well, you are just a child, and I am going to let you go back to your nuns. I am impressed with your truthfulness, but don't be surprised if you are called back in a few days. I have not decided how to deal with sixteen-year-old girls."

THE JEWISH BABY • Evidently, when Anna had caught the baby that was suddenly thrown at her, she did not yet understand that the baby was Jewish. Yet from Nonna's account of her interview at Gestapo headquarters, it seems as if this earliest of Anna's experiences in captivity—briefly caring for the baby and being accused by Dunja of intentional treachery—served to determine her last.

When I walked out of that building, I felt absolutely nothing; there was no fear, resentment, or anything. I felt absolutely nothing. I felt like a zombie that was moving, and that was about all. I don't remember anything about how I got back to the hospital.

BOMBING • About a month after Nonna's meeting with the Gestapo, on the night of October 22, 1943, several hundred British bombers attacked Kassel. They destroyed 90 percent of the city—leaving 10,000 people dead and 150,000 homeless—all in less than half an hour. Here Nonna gives the time span as fifteen minutes; later, she gives it as twenty-five (see Chronology). Nonna lived through the bombing of Kassel, but the hospital where she worked was severely damaged. Nonna wrote that the Gestapo building was destroyed.[1]

The bombing started at 7:45 p.m. and lasted fifteen minutes. By the end of those fifteen minutes, there was not much left of that big city except for thousands of bodies scattered around the city and near the bunker where I was. The bunker was adjacent to the main hospital itself. The main building of the hospital was burning, as were the homes around it. People were moaning and screaming for help, and the sky was red for many days to come. There was mass confusion for a long time. For me, I was so busy helping out in the bunker hospital working with the nuns and nurses treating those injured people who were not killed in the bombing that I lost track of time.

Several days later, when things had quieted down a bit, I remembered that I was supposed to be called back by the Gestapo. I was very concerned about what had happened, so a young girl who worked with me and I decided to walk outside and see what was left of the city. We walked over to where the Gestapo building had been and saw that there was nothing left of that wretched place. As I looked at the destruction around me, I thought that God had sent those planes to save me and that he had other plans for my life, so I managed to survive, alone.

• • •

POSTCARDS • Several photographs and postcards remain from Nonna's collection during this time. These are her captions to two of them, written after the war.

A village near Switzerland where the nuns and priest were trying to find a way to send Mama and me to live.

---

[1] http://en.wikipedia.org/wiki/Kassel, accessed January 26, 2009.

However, it was not meant to be. The Gestapo took Mama before we were able to move here.

Kings Theater, where the Gestapo forced Mama to perform concerts on the piano and the violin. They would take her from the concentration camp to perform and would take her back to the camp after her performances. This was all destroyed by bombs in 1943!

• • •

MEMORIES • Following are miscellaneous recollections and poems of Nonna's.

The nuns arranged for me to attend a parochial school (behind the cathedral) to complete my high school education. Mama and I sang in the church every Sunday, but this was all destroyed by the bombings in 1943.

• • •

I get homesick for my home, which long ago ceased to exist but will always remain in my memories. My young childhood years were very beautiful, and those memories that still live with me, and will live with me until death, have given me much comfort through the many years, especially when I feel sad or depressed.

• • •

I can hear my grandmother's command, which had a sound of love in it!
  I see it all as though it were only yesterday—it is all around me when I am alone!

I can live a life of fifteen years in only fifteen minutes.

I shudder with some of the sad memories (such as the death of my baby sister Taissia). I shall dwell only on happy memories and relive them sweetly over and over again.

To me, it was a dream so sweet, yet a nightmare so horrible, which will be with me always!

• • •

"WHERE ARE YOU NOW?" • Nonna had no idea what had happened to her mother. She just knew that on September 22, 1943, the Gestapo sent Anna away. In April 1947, Nonna wrote a poem to her mother. Following that are miscellaneous musings, from varying time periods.

TO MOTHER

O, Mother dear, where are you now?

Which road should I take, and where should I turn?

Am I the one to finish the journey

To freedom which we all have so yearned?

You gave me life and a happy childhood,

Though it only lasted for a while.

The memories will stay forever

Of those whom I so loved as a child.

As one by one they have been taken

From us by the terrors of war,

You have remained still so unshaken,

So brave and strong, though full of woe.

And as we almost reached the freedom

That we could see so clear by then,

They snatched you quite without reason,

And threw you into a lions' den.

I've mourned and cried while seeking answers

To what I could not understand,

Though we have suffered on this planet,

We shall embrace in Heaven's land.

• • •

MY MOTHER AND I

There are no words that can describe my beautiful,
loving, and so talented mother, who gave me so many
sweet memories that will last me a lifetime. She taught
me how to love, to care, to be generous and forgiving,
and many other qualities that build character.

[. . .] Unfortunately, since we both had traveled a long
and painful journey through the times during World War
II and the Holocaust, Mama was snatched by the Nazi
Gestapo at the age of 36 (still so beautiful and sweet)
and thrown into a concentration camp. There she was
destroyed—dying a horrible death—and leaving me to
be the lone survivor of my entire family.

[. . .] I am 70 years old, and I have tried to follow
all the teachings of my dear mother to be a strong and
caring person. I have a beautiful daughter of my own
now, and I only hope that I can leave her as much as my
mother left me.

When I was a very young child (4–5 years old), I
learned to recognize my mother's footsteps when she

came home from wherever she had been. I remember the sweet smell when she was around and the very gentle touches and embraces that would give me such a sweet feeling of security and love. I have been missing these for so many years since I lost her. However, those memories are with me always.

[. . .] My mother was indeed a lady of strength and a lot of courage, and also of many talents: playing the piano and violin, painting, and other things. But most of all she was very kind, forgiving, and generous to all those around her.

• • •

OBSERVATIONS

More and more, I am inclined to believe that the end is approaching, finally and irrevocably, though I am not sure how to explain this feeling, whether by my own approaching death or by the shadow of the future over our world in recent times. But whatever the future holds, I only hope that I do not live to see the final end with these mortal eyes.

In these days, the sense of approaching doom has spread down to the great mass of people. This is not only because of the brilliant way in which science has demonstrated its capabilities. I sometimes feel that science only provides a rationale for people's natural sense of dread at the work of their own hands, as witnessed by the sterile upsurge of philosophical pessimism that overcame the West after the second world war.

People sense it with all the pores and fibers of their

body and soul, the feeling that the end is not far off. The miserable wretches cannot wait to let themselves go: murdering thousands of ordinary people would give them the feeling of strength so coveted by the weak in spirit. They know that an executioner feels superior to his victim, gloating at the fear-dazed eyes and the trousers slipping down because his belt has been taken away.

The well-fed brute also likes to starve his prisoner. Nothing lowers the will to resist more than hunger. But when, in accordance with the law by which evil destroys itself, the executioners begin to murder their own kind, who until recently have interrogated, tormented, and killed "alien elements" (or sanctioned their killing "for the good of the cause"), then yesterday's "good comrades" suddenly disintegrate and, with cries of dismay, rush to prove themselves purer than the driven snow.

• • •

October 11, 1943

I remember Papa's words, which he frequently used at the beginning of World War II:

"When you are surrounded by enemies, it is through them that you have to seek refuge."

"When the friends are no longer there, we are forced to find refuge through the enemies."

"It is the enemies who are standing in our way, and it is the enemies who can show the way to refuge."

I believe that Papa was referring to some of the works of Leo Tolstoy. He read the works of this great Russian poet—especially during the years of 1939–41.

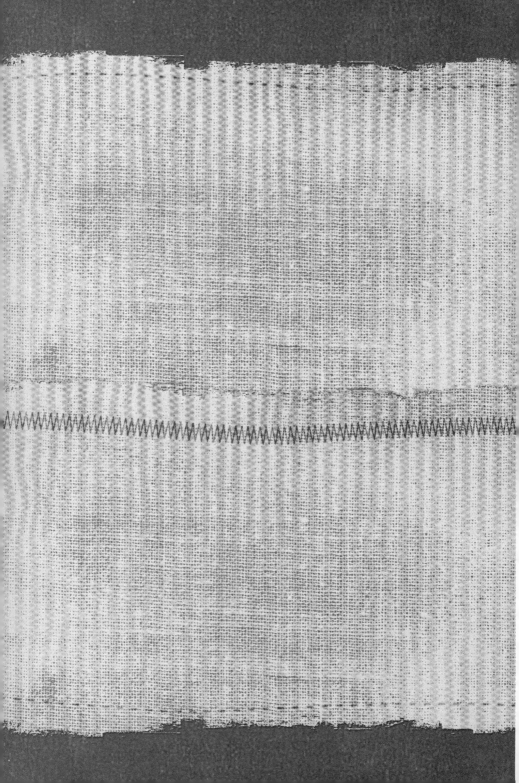

CHAPTER 37

SURVIVAL TO THE END

The walls of the hospital had been blown away. When I climbed up to look at where my room had been, I could look out into space. I moved to the bunker hospital—along with all the nuns, doctors, and patients—where the hospital continued to function. I was allowed to find a room along with the other employees on the upper floors of the bunker. There were quarters for the doctors and nurses and a cloister for the nuns, where there was a large Catholic chapel. Since there were no elevators, we all had to use the stairs to commute down to the bunker where we worked. There was a series of tunnels that had been built in a zigzag pattern to cut down on air pressure in the event of a direct bomb hit; these tunnels led us down to the hospital. I continued to work and live there until I started to develop health problems.

My first sickness started with a large swelling that developed on the left side of my neck—from my left ear to the middle of my chin. There was no pain associated with the knot, but I did run a low-grade fever and was very tired most of the time. However, I continued my education while working in the hospital. I was concerned about the way that I looked, and I tried to always wear a high collar to hide the knot.

As I was playing around with some friends, I jumped off of a table to the floor and heard something "pop" in my right side. It was so painful that I went down to my knees, and my friends rushed me to the doctor. He diagnosed it as a ruptured appendix, and I was immediately taken to surgery where Herr Dr. Hoffman removed my appendix. He installed drains in my side to let the infection come out through these drain tubes.

As a result of the ruptured appendix, I developed peritonitis and became a patient in the hospital where I worked. My friends and the nuns were very good to me and provided everything that I needed, including moral support.

All of this happened shortly after the Gestapo had taken my mother, so I was still very worried and concerned about Mama. I would watch the door and expect Mama to walk in at any time.

About four weeks after Mama had disappeared, I received a card of notification from the Gestapo that my mother was a prisoner; the card had been mailed from Concentration Camp Ravensbrück, located in Fürstenberg.

RAVENSBRÜCK • Located fifty miles north of Berlin, this concentration camp for women opened May 15, 1939. The overcrowded camp housed Jews, Gypsies, Poles, Russians, Ukrainians, and other political prisoners, including Germans. Records show that some 132,000 women entered

Ravensbrück between 1939 and 1945, with 50,000 women dying there. Nazis exacted slave labor, inflicting strict rules and grave punishment, even death. The Soviets liberated Ravensbrück on April 29–30, 1945.[2] Particularly given the Nazis' knowledge of the Jewish baby incident, Anna surely suffered severely at Ravensbrück.

This confirmed my worst nightmares that my mother was a prisoner, and there was no way I could help her. The postcard was very official, and it was mailed in October 1943. The card had my mother's prisoner number on the front—her number was 23893. These numbers were tattooed on the prisoners' arms, so there was no way out for her now that she was a marked woman. I cried my heart out, but my friends and the nuns were very supportive of me. They would encourage me to get well because that's what Mama would have wanted. After the initial shock had worn off and reality set in, I got mad and decided that I was going to get well and look for my mother.

TATTOO • Nonna might have been under a misconception, either at the time of the incident or when she recorded her memories. Bodily tattooing of prisoner numbers took place only at Auschwitz.[3]

I then developed rheumatic fever and became very sick. My joints swelled and were so painful that I could not even hold a pencil. I lost a lot of weight and became bedridden with the rheumatic fever. Within three or four weeks, I developed angina pectoris: the doctors diagnosed it as myocarditis, which had damaged the muscle in my heart. I was very sick for about two years, and when I recovered, I had to learn to walk again.

It was while I was sick and was a patient that I decided to

---

[2] Information from: http://www.jewishvirtuallibrary.org/jsource/Holocaust/Ravensbruck .html, accessed July 10, 2008.
[3] Laurence Rees, *Auschwitz: A New History* (New York: PublicAffairs, 2005), 65.

continue my education, and I studied to become a nurse. The nuns were tutoring me as well as the doctors: Dr. Rudolph Hoffman; Dr. Zahn, my cardiologist; and a young doctor named Ingrid Nubel. She became a dear friend to me—later her parents came from Düsseldorf and offered to adopt me.

It was early in the spring of 1944 (February) when I received the first letter from my mother. The letter had been written in German. I knew that Mama had dictated it because she used my pet nickname in the letter. It was a brief message; the Gestapo would only allow eight lines in a letter, and they censored every letter that went out from the concentration camps. The letter read as follows:

> *Dear Daughter Nonna:*
> *I am well. Do not worry! Stay well and wait for me.*
> *I kiss you, Krumchen.*
>
> *Your Mama, Anna*

The letter was written from the women's concentration camp in Ravensbrück, as was the first postcard. This letter was sent to the nuns at the Catholic hospital where I was being protected from the SS and the Gestapo. A Catholic priest who was in the KZ camps had arranged for this letter to be sent so I could hear from my mother. This gave me even more resolve to get well, even though I was heartbroken. If I had not had the nuns and my friends to support me, I am not sure that I could have handled this situation alone. I was very sick, but I never was lonely because my friends and the nuns would sit with me and read books and poems to me. I was unable to hold a book in my hands because the rheumatic fever had stiffened my joints.

They were also very painful. I studied almost constantly when I was not asleep, and this made the time pass a little more quickly. The doctors were trying to find a way to treat the rheumatic fever and myocarditis, but the only medicine that they were giving me was salicylic acid. They were also giving me therapy treatments.

FLOSSENBÜRG • This concentration camp in the town of Flossenbürg, Germany, incarcerated 111,000 prisoners between 1938 and 1945. About 73,000 prisoners died there. Malnutrition, lack of hygiene and medical care, and the brutality of SS guards caused most of the deaths at Flossenbürg. Nonna gave no reason why the Nazis moved Anna from Ravensbrück to Flossenbürg. The Second U.S. Calvary liberated Flossenbürg on April 23, 1945.[4]

I received another letter from Mama that was dated May 21, 1944, and was written on concentration letterhead from Flossenbürg Camp. This letter read as follows:

Dearest Nonna,

I am concerned about your health. How are you getting along? You are on my mind both day and night. You must take care of yourself and stay healthy. Don't worry about me. I am doing fine. Please write to me by whatever means that are available. Ask the Oberschwester or Sister Pia—or anyone that you can trust to write me. I need to hear from you, and for you to let me know how you are doing. Please send me two toothbrushes and a needle and thread and anything else that you can round up. Do not send luxuries such as chocolates, but I need soap, toothpaste, and if possible

[4] Information from: http://www.jewishgen.org/ForgottenCamps/Camps/FlossenburgEng.html, accessed July 10, 2008.

send socks, panties, and a warm cap. It is very cold here.
I am having trouble with my arms, but I am concerned
about everything, especially since I have learned that you
are having some health problems. Please write to me and
take care of yourself.

Kisses—Anna

I didn't know what Mama meant about having trouble with her
arms, but I learned later that the Gestapo had been using Mama
to entertain the "brass" by performing concerts both on the violin
and the piano. When she refused to perform because she was sick,
the Gestapo had broken her arms and, later, broke her fingers.
With the help of friends, the nuns, and Father Nikolas (the priest
who had been sent to the KZ camp), I was able to send packages
to Mama with some of the things that she asked for. I was deeply
worried about Mama and was so sad that she was going through
such tortures. I just didn't know how bad it was for her.

I received letters from Mama as follows: June 18, 1944;
August 6, 1944; and a letter that was started on August 22,
1944, and finished on August 29, 1944, but which was postmarked on September 3, 1944. Each letter was written in
German, and I knew that Mama was not able to write in the
German language. So I knew that she was having someone write
these letters to me. Each letter was inquiring about my health
and encouraging me to take care of myself. Mama expressed her
thanks to the Catholic nuns and the priest for taking care of me
and protecting me. In each letter, Mama would ask for potatoes,
dried bread (like Zwieback), and onions and any kind of food
that would not spoil. Schwester Gutegera, who was in charge of
the kitchen, always managed to get a few potatoes, onions, and

dried bread together, and I would have these packages sent to Mama through the priest (who had a few privileges).

I received a letter again that was written on October 1, 1944, postmarked October 3, 1944, in which Mama was not as positive and optimistic as she had been in her previous letters. She again asked me to please write to her and to keep her aware of my health situation. She would acknowledge the receipt of the packages and thank us for sending the food and other items to her. She also said that she had to hide her things under her bed because people were becoming desperate and would steal and even kill to survive.

PACKAGES TO ANNA • Prisoners were sometimes allowed packages, since the Germans provided so little. These possessions were the currency of the camps' black-market barter system.

It was some relief to get this correspondence from Mama because at least I knew that she was still alive, and this gave me some hope that we would find each other again when the war was over. My health was not improving, and the rheumatic fever was really taking its toll on me. The doctors were doing everything in their power to help me get well, but I continued to be very sick—I was still bedridden. The time passed slowly, and as I look back on it, I was so intent on getting well that I really didn't worry about the time that it would require.

I received the last card from Mama, dated April 11, 1945. The first thing I noticed was that her prisoner number had been changed from 23893 to 52234, and this was cause for horrible thoughts about what had happened to Mama.

CHANGED NUMBER • Anna's prisoner identification number would have been changed when she was transferred from Ravensbrück to

Flossenbürg. However, both Anna and Nonna seem surprised by the change, and they commented on it long after her transfer.

The card read as follows:

> *My darling daughter,*
>
> *I am writing this letter hoping that it will reach you. When you get this, it is possible that this will be the last communication from me. However, there is hope that the packages may still be arriving from you. The packages must carry this new number 52234—I can only guess about this new number. How are you doing? I am well and wait for at least one more letter with news about you from the Schwestern. It would be only fair to hear from you once more before it is all over. Write everything if it is possible.*
>
> *Your loving, loving mother*

The war ended officially on May 5, 1945, after the Americans arrived and freed the prisoners out of the prison camps. But it was too late for my mother. The Germans had known that they had lost the war but apparently decided that they would kill a few more people before the Americans arrived. How sad that my mother had endured and suffered so much, and came so close to surviving, yet was destroyed just days before she would have been free.

ODE • It is unclear whether Nonna wrote this poem in the early post-war era or much later, when compiling her transcription:

ODE OF MEMORIES

Be still my heart.

The thought is generous

Of those who are near you.

Why trouble those who care and love?

The past is gone and what is ahead

Is still to be felt.

The sun is bright,

The skies are blue,

It is no longer you who murmurs.

So, why do we feel the pain?

Perhaps of someone else who is near us.

But forgiveness is only an act,

Of much generosity and wisdom.

CHAPTER 38

LAST MESSAGE FROM MAMA

The last message from my mother came about four months after the war was over. A letter was left on my table beside my hospital bed by an unknown person or persons. The letter was scribbled on an old piece of paper and was folded into a small square. I never found out who left the letter, but my hands were bandaged and I could barely move because of the pain brought on by the rheumatic fever. I was also very sick with the ensuing myocarditis that had affected my heart, so a woman who was sharing my room in the hospital was kind enough to hold the letter so I could read it.

There was no date to denote when the letter had been written, but the letter was addressed to Nonna Lisowskaja. The first part of the letter was very hard to read since the first half of the page was written in Yiddish and Polish (not even good Polish). It was hard for me to understand since I could not or did not make out some of the words. But from my memory, the letter went something like this:

My dearest Kitten Nonnatchka—

(It was the name my mother called me when I was a small child, and I immediately knew that the message was not from anyone but Mama.)

It read on:

> *If this message will reach you, it will probably be the last one you will get from me and by God's miracle we will meet soon. Don't give up hope but if you don't hear from me within the next six months or see me after it is all over, please, my Koshechka, leave Europe as fast as you can. Don't waste time looking for me because you know that I would be coming to you first. Get away from Germany as far as possible. Your papa and I would want you to go to America, and that is where we would like you to settle. O God, I pray that you will stay well and alive. You are maybe the only one that is left, so remember to stay strong and have a lot of courage. I am also so very grateful to all the Sisters (nuns) who helped to keep you in a safe place and take care of you. May God bless them for protecting you from all the horrors. Love, love you for me and your papa, and all of us for eternity.*
>
> *Mamatchka (Mama)*

ENDEARMENTS • Anna's names for Nonna—*Nonnatchka, Kitten Non-natchka, Krumchen,* and *Koshechka,* as well as her own *Mamatchka*—all employ German diminutive endings and are derived from either the word for "crumb" or the word for "little cat."

At the bottom of Mama's letter, there was the following message, written in pencil and in large letters in Yiddish:

> *Anna was my very best friend, and I hope that you have as much talent as she did. Oh, how well she could play the piano and violin and sing. She also painted beautifully— she was a beautiful friend—and we loved her so. Anna fell and broke her arm, and they did not give her any treatment, but they still insisted that she paint and play the violin during the concerts held for the German "brass." Her arm became infected and your mother became very sick and was running a high fever from not having the proper treatment. However they continued to pressure her to play and to continue her painting. She developed gangrene in her arm and became very sick, but the Germans thought she was faking her sickness. They took her to the infirmary, where they broke her other arm and some of her fingers. She became sicker, and the general ordered her to be thrown into the incinerator. She was in shock and unconscious and was of no further use to them. Little one, don't wait for your mama—she only lived to see you again, and that kept her going for a long time. Do what she wanted you to do, and if I were going your way, I would love to meet you, but my destiny is a different road.*

It was signed "*S. I.*"

After I read the letter, it took me a few minutes to figure it out and to even realize that I was actually reading it at all. I fainted or blacked out, and the nuns told me three days later that I had suffered from severe cardiac seizures (cardiac arrest) and I spent those three days in the "last room" where they transferred dying patients. The nuns told me that they had taken it upon themselves to get the Catholic priest to give me the last rites of the Catholic Church, even though they all knew that I had been baptized in the Russian Orthodox Church when I was a baby.

When I tried to recall what I was doing before I passed out, I remembered the letter, which had disappeared—no one would tell me what had been done with it. I wish I had it now—and yet it might be just as well that someone had destroyed it or whatever happened to it.

Perhaps it might have put me in a condition from which I would not have survived until today. But I had to be strong and have the courage that Mama talked about. After a few weeks, I decided that I would get well, and I was mad enough to do it. After all, it was the last thing that Mama had wanted from me. However, there was always the hope that this was all a bad dream and that the last letter was someone's idea to leave it there for me as a cruel joke.

I began to watch for Mama. I had plenty of time since I was still bedridden and couldn't go anywhere. I just kept hoping that someday she would just appear—especially since there were a lot of people arriving from all kinds of KZ camps; I kept trying to seek them all out. The nuns continued to take care of me. I stayed in the hospital as a patient from 1945 through 1947 as my illness lingered and the doctors and nurses treated my rheumatic fever and myocarditis. I was completely bedridden and had lost a lot of weight. My muscles had atrophied, and I was unable to walk. However, with the skill, love, and care of the doctors and the nuns, I slowly recovered and received intensive physical therapy in order to be able to learn to walk again.

The nuns moved me into the cloister to protect me from the danger of being picked up by the Russian troops who had arrived in the area after the Americans had set everyone free. I had a Russian visitor come to the hospital, and he told me that he could arrange for me to go back to Russia and that I should prepare to be moved back. The nuns came to my rescue and told the Russian that I was dying and that if they tried to move me, I would surely die before they got me out of Germany. I knew that if they took me back to Russia I would be tortured or even put to death as a traitor for not retreating with the Russians at the beginning of the war.

• • •

POETRY • In May 1946, during her stay at the hospital while she recovered, Nonna wrote several "Little Thoughts." She later translated these "thoughts" into English and recorded them in her transcripts.

LITTLE THOUGHTS

Being the one of yesterday,

I veil myself in my illusions;

I manage to survive today,

The time of sorrows and confusions.

• • •

Embraced with thoughts and deepest feelings,

I ask myself, "Was it all real?"

Is there a chance that I have been dreaming—

The dreams too horrid to reveal?

• • •

I saw the Angel come from heaven.

He whispered softly in my ears,

"I have my wings, which are God-given,

You're safe beneath them. Dry your tears."

• • •

I never gave up hope that I would find my mother, and each day, I would hope that she would just appear. While I was recuperating, I had a lot of time to remember things as they were as a child when I was growing up, the love and the family that had provided a loving family unit. I thought a lot about Grandmother and would wonder what had happened to her after Mama and I left. As soon as I could move my fingers and hold a pen or pencil, I started to continue my daily diaries, and I wrote day and night.

I wrote my diaries in several languages—in case someone got them, he or she would not be able to read them all. My memories were surfacing faster and faster, starting with how I never had a chance to know Grandfather Yakov (Mama's papa). He was slaughtered by the Bolsheviks during the Revolution. His full name was Yakov Alexandrovich Ljaschov, and I thought about the chaos in Russia (World War I, combined with the Revolution). I wondered what life had been like for Grandfather Yakov. I never knew my grandfather on my papa's side of the family, who, along with the other members of Papa's family, lived in Warsaw, Poland. All my ancestors on my papa's side came from Poland. Of course, I never met any of them since I was born in the year 1927, long after things had changed, and there was no way to keep in touch with my family ancestors from Papa's side.

I was very fortunate to have known my grandmother (Mama's mother) and all of Mama's brothers and sisters. I received a lot of information from them, especially from my dear grandmother Feodosija Nikolayevna Ljaschova. My papa taught me as much as he could about his background, and with having the knowledge of Mama's family, I had an awful lot to remember and write about. There were a lot of photographs to go along with all that I remember.

I thank God for having such sweet memories from the first twelve years of my childhood life. I can write for many years to come and never finish all that I know. I thank God for all that was left for me by my family, who were all destroyed by the Revolution, World War II, and finally my mother by the Holocaust. I have survived by a miracle—becoming the lone survivor of my family.

• • •

WHY?

While my body was imprisoned,
My soul was free.
Now that my body is free,

My soul is restless.

How could this happen (or be)?
Have I not dreamed of total freedom?
The dream that stayed with me for years
I dream no longer—shed no tears.

Embraced with memories so vivid,
I suffer quietly alone.
There's no one left who shared my sorrows,
Who walked with me the road of horrors.

How many thoughts remain unspoken,
But memories can't fade away.
The horrors of the past still haunt me,
The ghostly shadows won't dissipate.

I tried to free myself, pretending it never happened.
Oh, what a fool I was in thinking I could easily forget.
My nights are long, my thoughts are lingering.
The past will always be with me.

No matter how I try, there's no escape from what was
    real.
Should I continue to reveal?
Should others learn the true life story
Of more than one who can no longer tell?

I am compelled to put everything into writing for those who do not know or refuse to believe the true story of what happened. There are not many of us left who know of those horrible times, and we must pass the knowledge on to those who should know the true history of all the horrors. It is the only way to keep such a thing from ever being repeated again. If we keep quiet and do not speak now about what happened before, it could surely happen again. One of my deepest regrets is that while I was bed-ridden with rheumatic fever at Marienkrankenhaus, someone broke into my trunk and removed the Hitler postage stamps from all my correspondence (probably to sell to some stamp collector). It is up to us survivors to be brave and let the whole world know all about the horrors that took place. We owe this to our children and the good God who, mercifully, let us live.

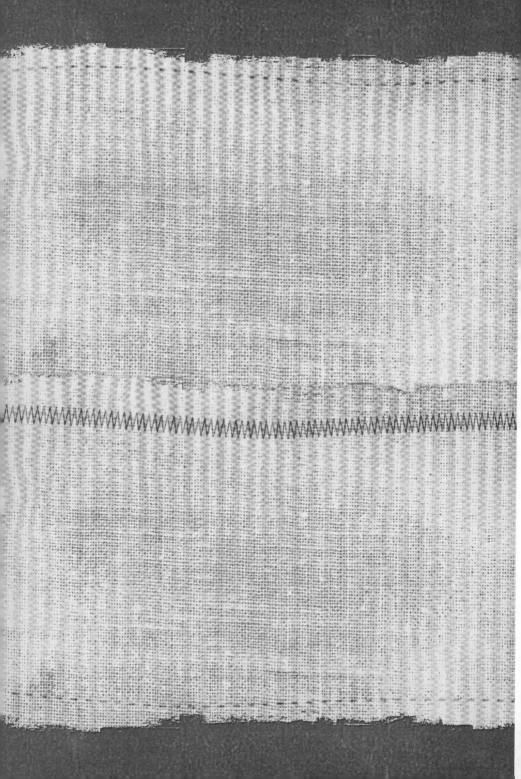

CHAPTER 39

SEARCHING FOR MAMA
Merxhausen Hospital

I learned that the Allies had opened a hospital approximately two hundred miles from Kassel where they brought a lot of people from the KZ camps to recuperate and receive treatment for all kinds of diseases—but most of them were being treated for starvation and the psychological disorders related to the horrors of the KZ. I wanted to be transferred to this hospital to continue my recovery, as it would allow me to continue to look for Mama. The nuns did not want me to go, but they understood my need to search for Mama. I talked to quite a few of the Allied officials about granting me a transfer to Merxhausen. Finally, there was a French doctor who arranged for me to be transferred from Marienkrankenhaus to Merxhausen. I had to be taken by ambulance since I was still very sick, but I made the trip without any problems.

When I arrived, I saw all those "friends"—which is what they meant and more—to me. There were a lot of them who had lost loved ones and who had survived by narrow escapes. Some of them were lone survivors of an entire family (like I was). I could identify with them, because I felt like I was the victim of the same horrors since I had lost the only precious relative that I had left—my mother.

The hospital was very busy, and each day there were new patients arriving for treatment. I would meet people as soon as they arrived, and I would show them Mama's picture, hoping that someone would recognize her and tell me some news about her. All of a sudden, I had a lot of people around me, and I was no longer alone. They were all suffering, the same as I was, and I felt like I had a large family now. They all just kind of adopted me, and when there were some happy times, the people always included me.

I was also there when there were sad times, like when Leja did not make it. I shared a room with her for a few weeks before she died. Leja was twenty-six years old; she had survived the horrors of the KZ camps only to die from the results of their horrors. She was like a sister to me, and I took it awfully hard, along with our many friends.

After Leja died, I asked to be transferred to the room of a lady who had suffered a stroke that had affected her speech and had left her paralyzed. She was confined to bed or a wheel-chair at all times. I cannot remember her first name, but her last name was Rosenbaum—so we called her Rose. When I showed her Mama's picture, she started to make loud noises and started to cry. She became so upset and shaken that the hospital staff had to give her a sedative—but she uttered a sound like she was calling Mama's name, Anna. I would not leave her side, hoping that she would start saying some words, or even one word. She had no relatives there, and since she could not speak or write, it was hard to communicate with her. We all loved her—she was our pet, and I took charge of caring for her as soon as they let me out of bed.

I shared the same room with Rose for three months, and then she died also—and we lost another loved one. Today, when I look at the pictures of Leja and Rose, the sadness still hurts.

It was 1948, and I had spent some time at Merxhausen. After meeting and talking with the Jewish prisoners and others from the KZ, I realized that I was never going to find my mother. I decided that I would finish my nursing education since I had quite a bit of training from the doctors and the nuns at the Catholic hospital. I moved to Bad Hersfeld, Germany, where I was accepted into the school of nursing. I was able to complete nursing school at Fulda, Germany, in just a few months. My grades were very high—I graduated with honors and was offered a scholarship to pre-med school in Heidelberg, Germany. From there, I was sent to work in the General Hospital of Hanau (Hanau was three kilometers from Frankfurt, Germany) for a short while.

After all my attempts to find Mama had failed, I finally realized (or accepted) that she really was gone, along with thousands of others, even after the Germans had lost the war. I finally accepted the fact that my mother had been thrown into the incinerator and burned alive and that the anonymous letter had been dictated by my mother just before she was killed by the Gestapo. All of this had happened just a few days before the death camps had been found by the Americans and the lucky survivors were freed.

"EVEN AFTER THE GERMANS HAD LOST" • On April 20, 1945, German guards evacuated, in a "death march," some fifteen thousand prisoners from Flossenbürg. When the Americans liberated the prisoners at Flossenbürg, on April 23, 1945, they found only two thousand prisoners alive in the camp.[5]

---

[5] http://history1900s.about.com/library/holocaust/blflossenburg.htm, accessed July 10, 2008.

New Life

CHAPTER 40

THE FINAL ARRANGEMENTS

Every survivor of this ordeal was anxious to get out of Germany and was making plans to get out as soon as possible. I left the hospital and took a job with the IRO Center of Hanau, Germany, as a secretary, and I worked for a woman by the name of Mrs. Hawksley, from London, England, who was in charge. I told Mrs. Hawksley that I wanted to go to America, and she arranged for me to apply for a visa. I had a friend (Zoya Wagner) who was an attorney and also helped me apply for the visa.

The process took something like two years to complete, giving me time to fully recover from my illness, make plans to leave Germany, and prepare for another long journey—to America. This would be a journey filled with promise and happiness for the opportunity to start a new life in a new country. Hope is a wonderful thing when one has been through the Holocaust and the horrors of war like I had been. This, after all, had been my father's dream for as long as I could remember—going to America.

IRO CENTER • Begun in 1946, the International Refugee Organization had an office in Hanau, Germany. Following the IRO's closing, a new relief organization was founded: the Office of the United Nations High Commissioner for Refugees, which is in operation to this day.

Before the visa was approved, I had to go through a lot of processing. I was required to appear before a lot of American and British authorities and to go through a lot of background checks. It was necessary for me to obtain and furnish verification about my mother and my family prior to being approved for a visa. At this time, the Germans had started a program to award money to the victims who had survived those terrible times, or to their families. My friend and attorney, Zoya, helped me organize all the documents, pictures, and proof of events that would make me eligible for some money from this fund (this was the first fund to be set up after the war for victims of the concentration and labor camps). There was much to be done, and the nuns had written me many letters stating that my mother had, indeed, been taken by the Gestapo and put into the KZ camps, from which she never returned.

There was someone else from that hospital who had been taken by the Gestapo and never returned: a Catholic priest. The only reason I could imagine was that he had helped some Jews, or whoever had been targeted by the Gestapo, by hiding them in the monasteries or in the hospital, much like the nuns had hidden me by moving me into their living quarters—even giving me a German name (Lena Schulz) to hide my identity. I was told to keep it a secret that they would tell whoever was curious about me and wanted to know why I was there that I was an orphan and that my home and family had been destroyed by the bombing during the war.

After getting all my papers together, I applied for the award money from the fund. I traveled to Wiesbaden, which is where the new German government was set up, headed by a chancellor. (I think it was Kohl.)

GERMAN CHANCELLOR • Nonna might have confused the chancellor's name with that of the current chancellor during the time of her writing. Helmut Kohl was chancellor between 1982 and 1998; the chancellor she refers to here must have been Konrad Adenauer, the new German government's first, who served from 1949 to 1963.

I had an appointment to appear before a panel of seven German men, who wore new uniforms and looked to be middle-aged. I was seated in front of a long conference table, and somehow I had a feeling that I was being interrogated again. It may have been my imagination, but I must say that I did not trust them. Their eyes were staring at me, and I did not feel comfortable.

After looking over my claims and documents, they asked me why I wanted to go to America. They asked me if I would accept an offer to stay in Germany, and they wanted to know if I would trade my visa for fund money. I told them that I just wanted to get whatever money was owed to me and that I would keep my visa to America. They offered me German citizenship and a scholarship to medical school if I would stay. I could see that they were trying everything possible to detain me and keep me in Germany. (I realized, years later, that they simply did not want me to go anywhere because I had in my possession proof that the Nazis had killed millions of innocent people and that the concentration camps had indeed existed.)

"DID NOT WANT ME TO GO" • Another interpretation of the Germans' reluctance to let Nonna leave is that they needed medical personnel, and having been trained in their system, she was valuable to them.

It was then I realized that those very people sitting across the long table from me in Wiesbaden were trying to protect themselves. These were probably ex-Nazis who did not care for us and were trying to make a new Germany. After they failed to talk me out of leaving Germany, they told me I could only get the fund money if I remained in Germany and accepted their offers. Again I told them that they could never talk me out of leaving Germany and that I would never give up my visa (and perhaps any of my papers and letters). I was one of the few left that had such papers and proof of the horrors they had created. They finally pulled out a piece of paper, which they made me sign, and gave me $1200. They told me that this was restitution and that the money was to pay for the trip and my troubles in appearing before them. They also told me that by accepting the $1200 in German money, I would release my claim for further attempts to collect for my mother.

By this time, I was somewhat angry, and all that I could think of was to get out of that place. I only had ten days left on my visa when I appeared before these men, and I had to get to Bremerhaven to catch the ship that would take me to America, where I planned to make a new life for myself. There was no money or anything that Germany could give me to not go to the country that my father had dreamed about for so many years to make his home.

• • •

REMEMBERING (EVEN NOW)

I am acutely aware of *all of it*!
I can hear the voices of those that I loved.
I can see the faces of those who are long gone.
I can travel through many places I have once traveled and see things as I saw them many years ago.
When I am alone, I see fragments of my past played before me!

• • •

I have always known that, being the only survivor of my entire family, I had done the right thing by leaving Europe—and that it would have made my father very happy. All the members of my family who had been so brutally murdered by Hitler, Stalin, and other such monsters would also be happy. This piece of history that I was a part of I do not want to forget, nor let anyone else forget. I will do my best, before I cease to exist, to tell all of those who do not want such horrible things to ever happen again. The truth shall live forever.

"THE TRUTH SHALL LIVE FOREVER" • Nonna climbed aboard the USNS *General W. G. Haan* before it sailed from Bremerhaven on May 20, 1950. She faced a severe storm during the long voyage. The bad weather delayed her travel, but she arrived at the Port of Embarkation in New Orleans, Louisiana, on June 6, 1950, and Nonna set foot on American soil. Her father's dream, for so many years, finally came true for Nonna.

OCTOBER 1989: AMERICANS

We are Americans,

You and I.

The land we are sharing

With its clear and friendly sky

Is a gift from God

For you and I.

Though times have been changing,

Nothing's the same.

The freedom is here

And shall always remain.

The clouds appear

But move on in the sky.

We are Americans,

You and I.

Afterword

DID IT REALLY HAPPEN?

by Nonna Bannister

Was it all as bad as what we learned from the ones who were there? Why is it so important for us—all of us—to know and remember what happened in the past? Perhaps our children and grandchildren will study the history of these things. All that is important enough to be put into the history books should be respected as the truth.

Just as we read and believe in the Great God Himself and Christ, who we believe was crucified for the cause of salvation of all who were created by God, we must not forget what happened to those who were tortured, tormented, and murdered by the hands of evil men. They (the victims) did not commit any crimes except that they were born and were just there in those troubled times. As the philosopher Santayana forewarned, "Those who cannot remember the past are condemned to repeat it!"

However, I believe forgiveness is important. It is to forgive, as God teaches us, but never forget—rather, to apply the truth to our lives in such a way that we do not repeat our sins over and over again. If we learn our lessons from the Word of God, who was the Creator of all, and if we believe in His Word as God's Word, we shall also be aware of all that happens while we are in His world.

Since we cannot turn back, but live our lives now and tomorrow and after, we need to be aware of evil things, which may always be with us until death. Death comes quickly, and we all will die sooner or later. But it is the life after death that fills us with great hope, and we should never be afraid of dying. However, if we learn how to survive even when we are faced with death, we become stronger and can live until God is ready to take us into eternity.

Appendix A

Life with Nonna

as told to the editors by Henry Bannister
Summer 2008

Henry Bannister met Nonna in 1951, after her ship from Germany arrived in New Orleans, Louisiana. They married shortly after her arrival in America, and their marriage lasted fifty-three years and fifty-three days—until Nonna's last breath. Henry and Nonna had three children.

Nonna was an intelligent, lovely woman. She was beautiful physically, emotionally, and spiritually. As brutal and horrifying as they were, her experiences in German-occupied Russia and subsequently in Germany in the midst of the Holocaust, only deepened Nonna's faith in God. This faith saved her from the bitterness many Holocaust survivors developed after the war's end. Love and compassion ruled Nonna's heart. With God's help she forgave those who purposely hurt her, as well as those—both Russian and German—who so cruelly slaughtered her family.

Nonna was a loving and faithful wife, mother, and grandmother during her marriage of more than five decades. When she decided to tell Henry about her Holocaust experiences—a few years before she died—she spoke without hatred, bitterness, or anger. She held on to her grandmother Feodosija's deep faith in God, and until her latest years she regularly worshiped in church. She was baptized in the Russian Orthodox church as a child and worshiped there; after the war, she became Baptist through the influence of American Baptist missionaries in Germany. The Napoleon Avenue Baptist Church of New Orleans, Louisiana, sponsored her emigration to the United States, and she worshiped in Baptist churches thereafter. Nonna also remembered her father's words about forgiving others. She forgave much, and her forgiveness kept her from a long life built on bitterness and revenge seeking.

But the Holocaust and the war impacted Nonna in several distinct ways not uncommon among Holocaust survivors. She became very private in her dealings with other people, wanting few friends. She was secretive about her life during the war years and about the fate of her maternal Russian and her paternal Polish families. Even Henry knew little about his wife until her final years. Only in the 1980s did she decide to share her experiences with Henry, to show him the diaries and photographs, and to describe the horrors and pain she and her family had endured at the hands of the Russians and the Nazis.

Nonna's habit of hiding this information was probably a combination of the natural reticence many Holocaust survivors experience and a carryover from the days when it was vitally important to hide valuables and personal papers from the Communists during her early years in Russia and from the Nazis during her Holocaust years. It is also likely that having experienced such harsh treatment, confiscation, and imprisonment at the hands of two governments, she no longer trusted government in general.

Even after the war, she sewed private papers, photographs, and documents into the linings of her pockets and the hems of her dresses or stashed them in other clever hiding places. Henry would see her writing on the yellow tablets and some-times look—in vain—for them while Nonna was away. She hid these in her trunk, and she locked that trunk inside a larger trunk. She kept other personal memorabilia hidden as well, inside the black-and-white-striped ticking pillow she had kept on her person throughout the Holocaust and postwar years, even hiding them from Henry again after finally showing them to him. Throughout her adult life, including hospital stays in the United States, Nonna slept with that pillow at her chest. She never went anywhere overnight without it.

After Nonna died, her children and Henry eventually found transcripts, photographs, documents, personal papers, childhood diaries, postwar diaries, and many other things that belonged to Nonna. Though they had to break the trunk's pad-lock, since Nonna had hidden its key too well, her family even-tually found almost everything—official visa information, travel baggage-claim slips, her mother's letters from Ravensbrück and Flossenbürg concentration camps, and photographs of her fam-ily and friends. But since Nonna's burial, the original Holocaust diary scraps have not been found again.

Henry knows that they survived the war and that Nonna kept them. She had translated and transcribed them word for word onto yellow legal pads in her later life, and Henry had typed that transcription for her. But though he and his family have searched everywhere for them, they have not been able to discover them. It is possible that Nonna sewed them into a secret pocket or lining of the ticking pillow, which was buried with her.

What happened to Nonna's family back in Russia, Germany, and Poland? Nonna's mother, Anna, died at the Germans' Flossenbürg concentration camp, probably in April 1945. Her last letter to Nonna was dated April 11, 1945. But Nonna didn't receive the letter until four months after the war.

Nonna last saw her maternal grandmother, Feodosija Nikolayevna Ljaschova, standing on the train platform in Konstantinowka, Ukraine, when she and her mother left for Germany on August 7, 1942. They never heard from her again. Nonna never returned to the Great House or to her home country.

Nonna last saw her brother, Anatoly, at the family reunion in Konstantinowka, Ukraine, in the late summer of 1939. After Anatoly left for St. Petersburg, Nonna and her family never heard from him again. She spent a lifetime searching for Anatoly. If Anatoly is still alive somewhere in the world, he would be eighty-four years old in 2009.

Most of Nonna's remaining relatives—aunts, an uncle, and cousins—had boarded a Russian train headed to Siberian safety and died when the trains were bombed.

Petrovich, caretaker of the Great House, went to the railroad tracks to pick up discarded coal during the spring of 1941. He never came home. Feodosija found his cart, still loaded with coal, abandoned by the tracks but saw no sign of him.

Nonna never met her father's family, who lived in Warsaw, Poland. Yevgeny lost contact with them during World War II, and they were never heard from again. Nonna never found out whether her father was Jewish.

Anna's good friend Taissia Solzhenitsyna died on January 17, 1944, from tuberculosis. Her son, Aleksandr "Sasha"

Solzhenitsyn, became "Russia's greatest living novelist," winning the 1970 Nobel Prize in Literature for *One Day in the Life of Ivan Denisovich*. Aleksandr joined the Red Army during World War II, achieved the rank of captain of artillery, and was twice decorated. For criticizing Joseph Stalin in a letter, he was imprisoned (1945–1953) in a Russian *gulag*—a prison in the Soviet system of labor camps. He was exiled from the Soviet Union in 1974. In 1984 he won the Templeton Prize for Progress in Religion. Aleksandr Solzhenitsyn was an active writer until his death during the publication of this book, on August 3, 2008.

Nonna Lisowskaja Bannister died on August 15, 2004. Her favorite flowers, lilacs, were out of season at that time of year, so Henry put roses on her grave, for she also loved roses. For her wedding, she had chosen pink roses for her bridal headpiece and worn a corsage of pink rosebuds.

Inside Nonna's coffin, next to her heart, Henry placed her black-and-white-striped ticking pillow—the pillow her grandmother had made for her and stuffed with the soft breast feathers of young Russian geese—the pillow that may still contain those tiny slips of soiled paper sewn together with a single thread—her Holocaust diaries. The pillow had been her constant companion in life. Henry knew she couldn't sleep without it.

Appendix B

"Is This It? Is This All?"

by John Bannister

As I reflect on my mother's life, many things are revealed to me that make sense now that she has passed on. Momma's attitude about life, especially challenges that she faced, was almost always positive. She had a very strong will to fight difficulties, a strong will to maintain her dignity, and a strong will to survive and move on. Reflecting on the kind of person she was makes it much clearer that her past had an indelible effect on what she would become. Why was she such a private person? Why did she not allow herself to get too close to people? Why was her family the most important thing to her? Why was she always such a realist regarding life and at the same time so compassionate toward others?

It can be understood that after enduring so much pain at an early age—witnessing such atrocious behavior and lack of civility, having nearly her entire family decimated—she would hold all of these pains inside for over four decades. Privacy was her way of coping with the past hell she had witnessed.

Although Momma loved being around people, loved doing things for others and giving of herself, she had very few close friends during her lifetime. I now believe that it wasn't because she was so private but rather because of her fear of getting close to others and then having them taken away from her. I recall many acquaintances, but only a few people she truly confided in and to whom she became as close as a sister.

To Momma, nothing was more dear or important than her family and her home. She worked daily to make sure we were cared for and loved. She was totally dedicated to serving her husband and creating the best home possible for her kids. Her home was the only place she could feel safe and secure, and it was her most important resource to draw on for true happiness.

Momma was always willing to listen to what you had to say, and she always put logic and realism into any advice she rendered. We all know that realism can sometimes come with a bit of a sting, but she would wrap it in compassion and make you feel loved, no matter the consequence.

Momma's love and admiration for Daddy were always evident, even when she may not have been happy with him about something. I believe that feeling was mutual between them. She was proud of her husband, not because of certain successes or accomplishments he may have achieved, but more for the type of man he is. Daddy has lived a life based on a strong work ethic, strong moral fiber, and dedication as a husband and father. These are the qualities Momma saw in Daddy when they met in 1951, and Momma felt truly blessed that God had sent a man like that to love her. They shared fifty-three years and fifty-three days together.

My mother would be very humbled and glad that her life story made it into a book. Once she decided to share her memories with her family, she was committed to the idea that no one should forget what happened to her and millions of others during a time in which, to those unwilling participants, a new level of horror was displayed. She wanted no one to forget that good always overcomes evil in the end. She hoped that the civilized world would never again allow hatred to spew so openly and then look the other way.

On August 15, 2004, at noon, as the church bells were tolling in Jackson, Tennessee, my mother's long journey on earth came to an end. She had lived through and witnessed more pain and suffering than any individual deserved. During the last few weeks of her life, she had mentally gone back in time and relived some of those terrible memories—back to the Nazi camps, back to the train ride to Germany, back to her father's murder. It was as if these horrors were happening all over again for her, and all we could do was pray and wait it out.

After about five days in that state, she came back around, and I will never forget her looking me straight in the eyes and saying, "Is this it? Is this all? Is this it?" I knew she understood that her time here was almost over and that she would finally be reunited with her Papa, Mama, Anatoly, and all her other loved ones.

Many beautiful memories and precious times were shared with Momma at the end, and although she still fought hard to stay here with us, her body succumbed to the natural result. No more pain and suffering, Momma; no more.

On behalf of the Bannister family, I would like to thank several special people who helped this project become a reality:

To Denise and Carolyn, for the love and respect you have shown to Daddy and for being so diligent to bring Momma's memoirs to life.

To my wife, Kathy, for all the time and care you spent sorting Momma's writings and pictures and for being supportive to Daddy.

To Greg Johnson, for seeing the value in telling Momma's life story to others and for your honesty with our family.

Appendix C

DOCUMENTS

MAP OF THE WESTERN SOVIET UNION • Nonna included this map in her transcript, with her own handwritten notes indicating, among others: "Leo Tolstoy's place," "Grandmother's birthplace," "Konstantinowka dacha, Great House," "Taganrog, Nonna's birthplace," "Rostov on Don," and "Novorossisk, Mama's birthplace."

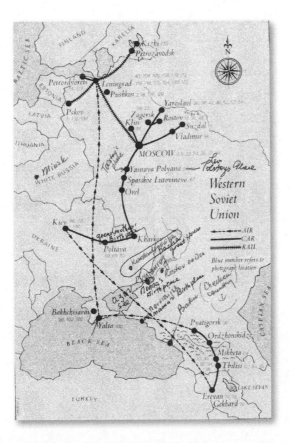

BIRTH CERTIFICATE • IRO-certified copy of Nonna's birth certificate.

Translation from Russian
                    Ukrainian

Registrar's Office Birth Certificate

Birth Certificate № 1205

Citizen N o n n a L I S O V S K A J A , Eugen's
daughter was born on Twenty second of September
nineteen hundred and twenty five (22.IX 1925)
    Inscription has been made on May 6,1942 sub № 1205.
Parents: Father: LISOWSKIJ, Eugen, the son of Ivan
         Mother: LJASHOWA, Anna, Daughter of Jakob
Birth place: Taganrog, District Rostow
Place of registr.: Office Konstantjinow ZAGS

    Seal   (Signature)
                Chief of Division

                (Signature)
                (Chief Clerk)
Registered on June 10,1942

Certified true copy:
Hanau/Main, June 23,1949

                        L.Kalve
                        Legal Counsellor
                        IP AC W 137, Hanau

IRO CERTIFICATE • Document from the IRO certifying Nonna's residence at the hospital in Kassel, Germany.

C e r t i f i c a t e ~ *extract.*

IRO HQ Area 1, Frankfurt/Main certifies, that

Miss Lisowskaja Nona, born on 22.9.1925 in Taganrog/Russia,

was legally resident on 1.1.1947 in Marien-Krankenhaus

at Kassel.

N. Shandra
Signature

Seal

Translation true:
Legal Counselor

Hanau, Feb. 21st 1950

Reg. No... 2893.

Nonna L. Bannister

MARRIAGE LICENSE • Nonna and Henry married on June 23, 1951.
Their photograph, taken as they cut their wedding cake, appeared in *The
Journal,* the local newspaper. In that article Nonna listed her birthplace
as Frankfurt, Germany. She kept her Russian/Ukrainian heritage a secret
even from her family for many years.

STATE OF LOUISIANA, } EIGHTEENTH JUDICIAL DISTRICT COURT, 193
PARISH OF WEST BATON ROUGE } CLERK'S OFFICE

TO ANYONE AUTHORIZED TO CELEBRATE MARRIAGES IN SAID PARISH OR STATE—GREETING:

You are hereby authorized to join in marriage according to law_____ – William Henry Bannister –
and_____ – Nonna Lisowskaja – _____, there appearing no lawful cause of impediment to same.

Given under my hand and seal of said Court, at West Baton Rouge, this____17th____day of____June,____
A. D. 1951____
10:00 A.M.   Elsie Wm. Lefebvre   Clerk.

I, _a minister of the Gospel,_ hereby certify that I solemnized the RITES OF MATRIMONY
between _William Henry Bannister_ and _Miss Nonna Lisowskaja_
on the _23_ day of _June_ 19_51_

THREE WITNESSES SIGN: THE MINISTER AND PARTIES SIGN:
                                          William H. Bannister
                                          Nonna Lisowskaja
                                          Charles T. Nally, Jr. Pastor
                                          Victoria Baptist Church

LETTER TO HENRY

Nov. 22nd, 2001

My Darling this is the day which everyone has some Thanks to give. So, Happy Thanksgiving to you my Darling!! and I cannot find anything to thank for more than to thank God for having you by my side. To thank you for everything you have done for me for the over 50 yrs. that past. And you are still doing things for me and comfort me in such way that it is not possible for me to express my feelings by just writing these few words. I have many things to thank God for but you are the most important and biggest thing for me to thank Him. So, my Love, I just want you to know just how much I love you and will always Love you till the end.

Love Nonna or just Me

COMMEMORATIVE CERTIFICATE

50th Anniversary
Marriage Certificate

STATE OF TENNESSEE **COUNTY OF SHELBY**

I, Jayne S. Creson, Clerk of the aforesaid, do hereby certify that the Rites of MATRIMONY were solemnized

between Nonna **and** Henry Bannister

on the 23rd **day of** June **19**51.

Given under my hand and official seal at Memphis, this

the 23rd **day of** June 2001.

Jayne S. Creson

Shelby County Clerk

LETTER FROM HENRY • This was one of Nonna's last notes from Henry. She died just over a year later, fifty-three days after their fifty-third wedding anniversary.

OUR 52ND ANNIVERSARY

June 23, 1951-------- I loved you then!

June 23, 2003-------- I still love you now!

In many ways, it does not seem that it has been 52 years since we were married. The time has flown quickly as we raised three fine children even though we have had many good times and a few not so good times. However, *we have been there for each other* through the good and through the bad.
As we get older, our love seems to grow as though we are one and I want to thank you for loving me and being my "soul" mate through all these years. It was God's will that sent you to me from a far away land----so I feel that it was God's plan for you and I to share our lives together. I know that we have more years together and I want you to know that I love you with all my heart.

HAPPY ANNIVERSARY
WITH
LOVE

Henry

Appendix D

GENEALOGY OF
NONNA LISOWSKAJA BANNISTER

NONNA'S FATHER'S FAMILY
Paternal Grandfather: Johan Stanaislaus Lisowsky
Paternal Grandmother: Wanda (maiden name unknown)

Known children of Johan and Wanda:
    Yevgeny Ivanovich Lisowsky (Nonna's father), b. 1897
        in Warsaw, Poland
    Stanislaw Lisowsky

NONNA'S MOTHER'S FAMILY
Maternal great-grandfather: Alexander Alexyevich Ljaschov
Maternal grandfather: Yakov Alexandrovich Ljaschov
Maternal grandmother: Feodosija Nikolayevna Ljaschova

Children of Yakov and Feodosija:
    Ivan (Vanya)
    Xenja
    Anna (Nonna's mother)
    Leonid (Ljonya)
    Antonja (Tonja)
    Yevgeny (Zhenya)

NONNA'S FAMILY

Anna Yakovlevna Ljaschova, b. 1906 in Novorossisk, Russia;
m. Yevgeny Ivanovich Lisowsky, b. 1897 in Warsaw, Poland

Children:

    Anatoly (b. 1925, last seen in 1939) Yevgeny

    Nonna (b. 1927, d. 2004) Yevgenyevna

    Taissia (b. 1940, died in infancy in 1940)

• • •

William Henry Bannister, b. 1927 in Bogalusa, Louisiana;
m. Nonna Yevgenyevna Lisowskaja

Children:

    W. H. (Hank Jr.) Bannister

    Elizabeth J. (Bannister) Sumner

    John D. Bannister

Chronology

Nonna wrote a chronology, including German and Russian national history along with her personal one, to which a few additions have been made. It begins in the late 1800s with the birth of her father and ends when she sets foot on American soil to begin a new life. Though some of the information has been covered in other places, its inclusion here reflects the events Nonna particularly wished to make known. Editorial additions appear in italics.

1897: JANUARY 8

Yevgeny Ivanovich Lisowsky (my father) is born in Warsaw, Poland. His father, Johan Lisowsky, and mother, Wanda (last name unknown), were wealthy landowners around the Warsaw and West Ukraine areas, which were still occupied by Poland.

1906: DECEMBER 24

Anna Yakovlevna Ljaschova (my mother) is born in Novorossisk, a city near the Black Sea (Caucasus). Her father, Yakov Alexandrovich Ljaschov, and mother, Feodosija Nikolayevna, were owners of at least seven dachas with grain mills and orchards throughout the southern parts of the Ukraine and southern Russia, with most of them located near the Black and Caspian seas.

Yakov's holdings were vast, and at each property there were hired hands to take care of the house and lands when the family was away. Their favorite place was in Konstantinowka, where they had a thirty-seven-room house referred to as the Great House. Whenever possible, the entire family gathered at the Great House for Christmas and other celebrations.

1907
Yakov Alexandrovich Ljaschov is accepted into the Imperial Cossack Army.

In doing so, he follows in the footsteps of his father, Alexander Alexyevich Ljaschov, who had been a count and also a Cossack. Alexander fought in the war with the Tatars around Odesa near the Azov Sea, and he was killed in the war somewhere near Odesa. His son, Yakov Alexandrovich Ljaschov, was to become Nonna's grandfather.

1909–1910
Yakov becomes a member of the Imperial Protection Unit and is honored by Nicholas II as a faithful servant to the Tsar.

Nicholas II, last Tsar of Russia, sends Yakov a postcard saying, "Mother Rossija is bleeding." The card, along with other family photos and documents, was hidden in a small pillow Nonna wore around her waist during the Holocaust and was brought to America in 1950.

1916
Yakov assumes a post with the Imperial Guard.

As a trusted staff member, he is to protect the Tsar and his family.

1917: SPRING
Yakov is engaged in transporting people of some influence out of the troubled areas of Russia, which were hit hard by the Revolution.

1917: FALL
The Revolution reaches its peak.

Everything in Russia is in chaos. Yakov and Feodosija make plans to flee Russia by sailing from the Black Sea to Romania or some other safe place.

1917: LATE FALL
Yakov Alexandrovich Ljaschov is slaughtered by Bolsheviks while on duty transporting people by train.

1917: LATE NOVEMBER
Feodosija Nikolayevna and her six children receive the tragic news of Yakov's death from his best friend, Dimitry Ivanovich, who encourages her to take the family and flee to Novorossisk. With his help, the family travel to Ukraine, where they have a dacha with an orchard. The village was called Santurinowka (later, Konstantinowka).

1918
Arrangements are made to send Anna to the university in St. Petersburg to attend an institute for gifted young girls, to study music and art.

Yevgeny Ivanovich Lisowsky and his brother, Stanislaw, enroll at the University of St. Petersburg. The arrangements are made by Yevgeny's oldest sister's husband, then a professor of physics at the university. Yevgeny's sister and her husband lived in Riga, Latvia; her husband was Latvian.

1918–1921
Yevgeny studies physics, art, and languages. His brother, Stanislaw, studies chemistry and physics.

1922
Anna (age sixteen) and Yevgeny (age twenty-five) fall in love, and Yevgeny remains in St. Petersburg while his brother, Stanislaw, returns to Poland.

1923: SPRING
Anna and Yevgeny travel to Santurinowka to ask Feodosija Nikolayevna's permission to get married.

1923: SUMMER
Anna and Yevgeny marry at the Orthodox church, with Feodosija signing a consent.

1923: LATE SUMMER
Yevgeny makes an attempt to move Anna and her family out of Russia and into West Ukraine but does not succeed.

1924
Another attempt to move Anna's family, this time to Poland, fails.

1924: DECEMBER
Anna and Yevgeny decide to move to Taganrog (near the Sea of Azov) to a house that belonged to Feodosija's family and was vacated when they moved to Poltava.

1925: NOVEMBER 3
A son, Anatoly, is born to Anna and Yevgeny.

1927: SEPTEMBER 22
A daughter, Nonna, is born to Anna and Yevgeny.

1928
Yevgeny makes contact with the Romanian friend he had met while studying at the University of St. Petersburg. They arrange several meetings in attempts to establish some communication with the Polish government.

1929: SUMMER
Yevgeny and his Romanian friend make another failed attempt to move to Poland (this time only Yevgeny's immediate family).

1929: EARLY FALL
Yevgeny accepts a position as an interpreter for foreign visitors to the largest machinery factory in the city of Rostov-on-Don.

1929: LATE FALL
Yevgeny and Anna move to Rostov-on-Don. There they are provided with a roomy apartment near the machinery factory and close to the housing of foreign visitors. The apartment is located about one and a half miles away from the largest park in the city of Rostov, which was called Park of Rest and Culture.

1930
Anna makes new friends and engages in music and art competitions. Yevgeny and Anna attend many parties and surround themselves with a circle of cultural people. They attend the Theater of Rostov regularly.

1931
Yevgeny invents a machine that slices sugar cones into cubes.

1931–1932
Anna leads a very busy social life, giving piano and violin concerts. She also paints constantly.

1932
Yevgeny demonstrates his invention at the factory's banquet with many foreigners in attendance, and he is presented an award by a German representative.

1933
Yevgeny and Anna make friends at the University of Rostov, and Yevgeny takes on some extra jobs repairing some of the university's medical and laboratory instruments.

1933–1934
We travel to Nachichevan, where the university was located, quite often. We went by streetcar, about a thirty or forty minutes' ride. It was then that I believe we became acquainted with Aleksandr Solzhenitsyn, who had been studying in the chemistry department at the university. (It is only to the best of my recollection.)

1935
Rumors of war spread throughout Russia. Yevgeny keeps in close touch with foreigners from the Western countries. He receives much news from Europe. We have visitors to our apartment quite often, and I could never understand what the conversations were about. They were spoken in several languages.

1935–1936
Russia prepares for warlike situations. Children in school have drills about what to do in case of the enemy's attack. Planes fly over, dropping fake "chemical bombs." People are encouraged to dig shelters in their yards. Air-raid-alert sirens are installed in all the neighborhoods, and occasionally they are turned on in exercise and practice drills.

1936–1937
Yevgeny and Anna take the rumors of war seriously and decide that it would be beneficial to move to Santurinowka, which by then had been

annexed to the town named Konstantinowka, Ukraine. Plans are made to move in with Feodosija while the house there is being divided into apartments. Other members of the Ljaschov family are heading back home also. Yevgeny thinks it is a good idea to be closer to West Ukraine and Poland in case war breaks out.

1937
The members of the Ljaschov family move back to the Great House with its thirty-seven rooms, four kitchens, and stable for six horses.

1937–1938
Yevgeny and Anna open a photography and portrait studio in Konstantinowka. Anna engages herself in working at the "Little Theater" at the Civic Club (next to the studio). They also organize a music school for young girls at the club.

1938
Yevgeny travels to Yalta in the Crimea (a resort area on the Black Sea), where he meets his Romanian friend again in an effort to get out of Russia. This time he is willing to make an attempt to get to Romania.

Yevgeny receives the discouraging word from his friend that emigration to Romania is impossible. (It all seemed so hopeless.)

1939
Germany invades Poland. World War II is on. All communication with the West ceases. The Russians become suspicious of anyone who makes even the slightest contact with the outside world. Grandmother dismisses all the hired hands except Petrovich, whom she claims is a relative.

Yevgeny makes arrangements to take Anatoly to St. Petersburg (Leningrad) to attend school and stay with relatives.

1939: LATE SUMMER
Anatoly is brought home for his last visit with the family by Grandmother's brother from Riga, Latvia. The family is in an emotional and confused state. I do not understand any of their plans. Yevgeny and Anna, for the first time in their marriage, are faced with great emotional outbursts. I am confused and frightened. Anatoly leaves, and we never see him again.

1940

Anna is with child and has a difficult pregnancy because of an attack of malaria. Her fever attacks grow frequent, and she spends a lot of time in bed.

1940: AUGUST 29

Anna gives birth to a baby girl. She names her Taissia.

1940: SEPTEMBER 3

The baby dies of hepatitis as a result of Anna's malaria attacks during her pregnancy.

1941: SUMMER

The war is now on Russian soil. All young, able-bodied men are drafted into the army. Jews from Poland flee to Russia and the Ukraine, and they are being transported to Siberia.

Russians begin evacuation of those who want to go farther east. The trains are loaded every day. People are in great confusion. Many do not wish to be evacuated and want to remain behind.

1941: EARLY FALL

German planes bomb Konstantinowka frequently. The Germans approach. The Russians move out, burning and destroying much behind them.

Yevgeny decides to remain behind and plans to go into hiding until the Germans arrive.

1941: LATE FALL

German soldiers move into Konstantinowka. They are searching homes and cellars for food. They are cold, hungry, and desperate.

Anna and Nonna sought out deserted homes in the next village, staying for indefinite periods of time and searching for food themselves, while Feodosija and Yevgeny stayed behind in the Great House.

1941: NOVEMBER

Drunken German soldiers find Yevgeny hiding in the cellar. They brutally beat him and pluck out his eyes.

1941: DECEMBER 12
Yevgeny dies from the injuries sustained during the assault.

1942: EARLY SPRING
Anna and Nonna move back with Feodosija into the family's Great House.

1942: SUMMER
Anna and Nonna engage in singing at the Orthodox church and move downtown in Konstantinowka to be closer to the church.

1942: LATE SUMMER TO EARLY FALL
The Germans offer to transport some Ukrainians and Russians to Germany to work in the factories because of the shortage of manpower there. Anna and Nonna decide to volunteer to be transported to Germany. Because of the age restrictions made by the Germans, Anna is forced to make quick arrangements in changing Nonna's and her own birth certificates. The year on Nonna's birth certificate is changed from 1927 to 1925, thus making her appear to be sixteen years of age; Anna's birth year is changed from 1906 to 1909, making her under thirty-six. (The Germans had set the qualifying ages between sixteen and thirty-five years.)

1942: FALL
Anna and Nonna journey by freight train through the Ukraine and Poland and into Germany under poor conditions and heavy guard by German soldiers. (Any attempt to escape from this journey was foiled.) These train cars were packed with people like sardines in a can. There were two SS men and two dogs assigned to guard each car.

1942–1943
Anna and Nonna are assigned to work in a carton factory in Kassel, Germany, and reside at a labor camp known as *Ostarbeiterslager* (a labor camp for workers from the East).

After a short stay there, they were transferred to a porcelain factory and back again, then to a textile factory.

1943: SPRING
Anna and Nonna are transferred from the factory to a Catholic hospital known as Marienkrankenhaus, in Kassel, Germany. Nonna is given a job as

an interpreter, and Anna is put to work as a nurse's helper. They are put to work in a section of the hospital built specially for foreigners from labor camps and prisoners of war; there are five barracks set up as a hospital next to the main building.

1943: LATE SUMMER

Anna and Nonna are transferred to the German hospital quarters because of conflicts Anna had with one of the Russian doctors.

The nuns of the Catholic hospital transfer Anna to work in the German hospital's isolation ward for communicable diseases such as diphtheria and scarlet fever. Nonna and her mother share a room in the upper floor of the hospital. Nonna is given the responsibility of all clerical work in the admitting office of the foreign hospital.

1943: SEPTEMBER 22

Anna has to appear before the Gestapo authorities and does not return.

Nonna visited Gestapo headquarters a few days after Anna's disappearance.

1943: OCTOBER 22

Kassel is bombed by British planes and is completely destroyed in a matter of twenty-five minutes. (The exact time was 7:45 p.m. to 8:10 p.m.) Thousands are dead, and everything is burning and in rubble. The Gestapo building is destroyed. All those in the hospital survive by being in the largest bunker in Kassel, which was built by French prisoners of war and was located at the back of the hospital and connected by an underground tunnel.

1944

After four months of not knowing Anna's whereabouts, Nonna receives notice from a concentration camp in Bohemia that Anna is imprisoned there. The reason for her imprisonment is not given.

Several letters from concentration camps arrive at intervals of four to six weeks. All letters are written for Anna in German by another person since Anna cannot write in German. Anna's prison number is stated on the letters, which were very carefully screened by the authorities.

1945

World War II comes to an end and the Americans take over Kassel, freeing all the people in the labor camps.

Four weeks before the war ends, Nonna comes down with rheumatic fever and myocarditis (an inflammation of heart muscle).

Anna died just weeks before her camp was liberated. Nonna received her final letter in September but continued to hold out hope of finding her.

1945–1947
Nonna's illness lingers for almost two years. While in the hospital, Nonna makes all possible attempts to find her mother.

1947–1948
After all the efforts to find Anna fail, Nonna asks to be transferred to a hospital in Merxhausen, Germany, where all the victims from the concentration camps—mostly Jews—are being taken. There she hopes to look for some clues about her mother.

1948
After spending some time in the Merxhausen hospital and meeting many of the Jews and other people from KZ camps, Nonna fails to find any clues about her mother. She decides to leave that hospital and travel to Bad Hersfeld, Germany, where there was a camp for refugees and displaced persons.

Shortly after arriving at Bad Hersfeld, Nonna makes arrangements to attend a nursing school in Fulda, Germany.

1949
Having acquired much experience and knowledge of nursing while with the German hospital in Kassel, Germany, Nonna finishes her nursing course in only a few months and graduates with honors. She receives a scholarship to a pre-med program in Heidelberg and travels there to enroll. But she decides to apply for a visa to go to America.

After working as a nurse in Hanau's general hospital for a short period, Nonna goes to work as a secretary at the IRO center in Hanau. She is employed by an English woman named Mrs. Hawksley, from London.

Mrs. Hawksley arranges for Nonna to apply for a visa to emigrate to the United States of America.

1950: EARLY SPRING

The visa is approved, and Nonna goes through the procedures required of all immigrants to the United States of America. The sponsor is the Napoleon Avenue Baptist Church of New Orleans, Louisiana. The place of employment and a residence are provided by church members—the Guillory family.

1950: MAY 5

Nonna goes to Bremerhaven, Germany, and awaits her departure by ship.

1950: MAY 20

The USNS *General W. G. Haan* arrives in Bremerhaven, and Nonna goes aboard ship.

1950: JUNE 6

The *General Haan* arrives in New Orleans at the Port of Embarkation, and Nonna leaves the ship, setting her feet on American soil.

Her father's dream for so many years finally becomes a reality for Nonna, the lone survivor of the family.

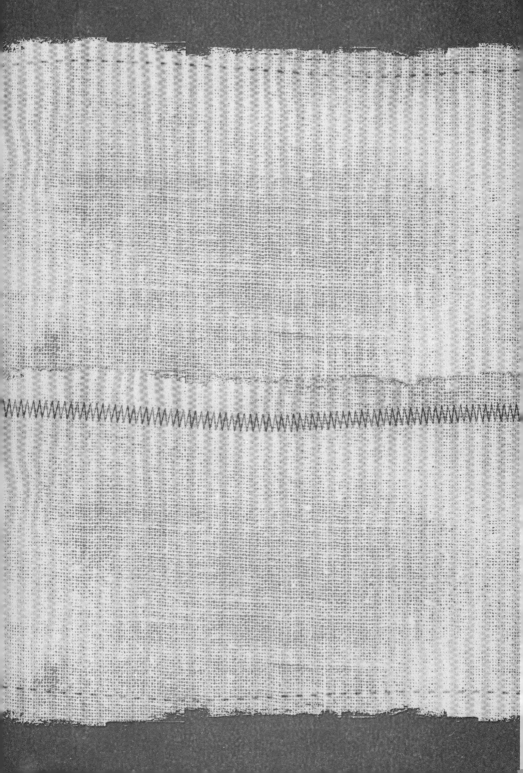

Glossary of Names and Places

The following list includes names of Nonna's family and friends up until 1950, as well as names of places that were part of her family history before, during, and after World War II.

Towns and villages are listed here with the country to which they belonged during that time, though borders have since changed in many places.

Feodosija and Yakov owned seven dachas in Russia and the Ukraine, which accounts for the different birthplaces of their children.

Babushka
Russian word for grandmother; Nonna's name for Feodosija.

Buchenwald, Germany
Location of the porcelain factory where Nonna and Anna worked for three months.

Dunja
Russian woman who reported Anna for trying to save a Jewish baby on the train to Germany.

Flossenbürg, Germany
Location of the concentration camp where Anna died.

Ivanovich, Dimitry
Family friend who helped Feodosija and her children escape after Yakov was killed.

Kassel, Germany
Location of the carton factory where Anna and Nonna worked for six months.

Nonnatchka, Kitten Nonnatchka
Nonna's nicknames.

Konstantinowka, Ukraine
Location of Feodosija's Great House. The place where family gathered for holidays and special occasions. Same town as Santurinowka, later in history.

Lichtenau, Germany
Location of a labor camp where Anna and Nonna worked for three months.

Lisowskaja, Taissia
Nonna's sister, born in 1940. Died at five days old.

Lisowsky, Johan Stanaislaus
Yevgeny's father, Nonna's paternal grandfather.

Lisowsky, Yevgeny Ivanovich
Nonna's father, born in Warsaw, Poland.

Ljaschov, Ivan (Vanya)
Anna's brother, a test pilot, killed in a plane crash in the Azov Sea.

Ljaschov, Yakov
Anna's father, Nonna's maternal grandfather. A Russian Cossack who was killed by the Bolsheviks during the Revolution. Born in Poltava, Russia (near Odesa).

Ljaschov, Leonid (Ljonya)
Anna's brother, born in Dnipropetrovs'k, Russia (now Ukraine).

Ljaschov, Zhenya
Youngest of Anna's brothers, born in Konstantinowka, Russia.
Served in the underground during the beginning of Hitler's
invasion.

Ljaschova, Anna Yakovlevna
Nonna's mother, born in Novorossisk, Russia.

Ljaschova, Antonja (Tonja)
Anna's sister, born in Sevastopol, Russia (now Ukraine).

Ljaschova, Feodosija Nikolayevna
Anna's mother, Nonna's maternal grandmother. Born near
Odesa, Russia (now Ukraine).

Ljaschova, Xenja
Anna's sister, born in Tashkent, which was then under Russian
protection (now Uzbekistan).

Marienkrankenhaus
German hospital run by Catholic nuns, at which Nonna and
Anna worked.

Nachichevan, Russia
City near Rostov-on-Don, location of the university Nonna
occasionally visited.

Nathan
Jewish boy who saved Nonna's life en route to Germany.

Nicholas II
Last Tsar of Russia. Nicholas; his wife, Alexandra; and their
five children were killed by the Bolsheviks in 1917. Nonna's

family has a birthday card sent to Yakov from Nicholas, postmarked January 1913.

Petrovich
Keeper of the Great House estate.

Ravensbrück, Germany
First concentration camp to which Anna was sent alone.

Rostov-on-Don, Russia
City where Nonna and her family lived and where Anna participated in the theater.

St. Petersburg, Russia
City where Anatoly was sent for his safety and education. Anna and Yevgeny were educated at the University of St. Petersburg.

Solzhenitsyna, Mrs. Taissia Shcherbak
Mother of Aleksandr Solzhenitsyn. Shared Anna's love of music.

Taganrog, Russia
City near the Black Sea; Nonna's and Anatoly's birthplace.

USNS *General W. G. Haan*
Ship that transported Nonna from Germany to the port of New Orleans in America, May 1950.

About the Author

Nonna included this "About the Author" page in her transcript.

MOST IMPORTANT IN MY LIFE
My husband, Henry; my children; and my grandchildren

THINGS I LOVE
To listen to music, read books, and write.
To play chess—I learned to play at a very early age, five
or six years old.
To paint—I used to paint when I was younger but have
not done so in a long while.
Classical music, opera, the symphony, concerts, ballet,
stage plays, the works of good artists (paintings), and
literature—I love to read good books.
To meet new people and make lots of friends.
All my grandchildren—Catie, Cristen, Zachary, Benjamin,
and Kara.
To have my immediate family around the table and laugh
a lot, remembering some of the funny and even silly
things.
To laugh a lot—my two sons and my daughter and
Henry have a great sense of humor. So do I!

MY FAVORITE COMPOSERS
Peter Tchaikovsky (especially his *1812 Overture*),
Beethoven, Schumann, Mozart, Bach, Chopin, and
others—too many to name.

MY FAVORITE OPERA SINGERS
Luciano Pavarotti (tenor) and, of course, my mother,
as I remember her singing when I was a child.

MY FAVORITE BALLET DANCER
Mischa (Mikhail) Baryshnikov, especially in *Swan Lake*.

MY FAVORITE PIANIST
Vladimir (Volodya) Horowitz—his last concert was held
in Moscow, Russia, in 1986.

MY FAVORITE ARTISTS
Rembrandt and Repic, and the works of most artists.

MY FAVORITE WRITERS AND POETS
Leo Tolstoy
Aleksandr Solzhenitsyn
Aleksandr Pushkin (the greatest poet I know)
Anton Chekov
Charles Dickens

I know much about Anton Chekov—he was born and lived
on the same street on which I was born, in Taganrog on Azov.
I know much about Aleksandr Solzhenitsyn—when I was five
years old, my mother and I spent the night at his mother's home
in Rostov-on-Don. His mother and my mother gave concerts

together (piano and violin). At the age of six I danced (ballet) the "Tatar Dance" at one of his mother's parties. They lived near the "Great Theater" in Nachichevan, which was near Rostov. My memories of those times are so vivid, and I visited the university where he attended very often.

HOROWITZ'S LAST CONCERT • Nonna refers to Horowitz's last concert in Russia. His final concert took place in Hamburg, Germany, in 1987.

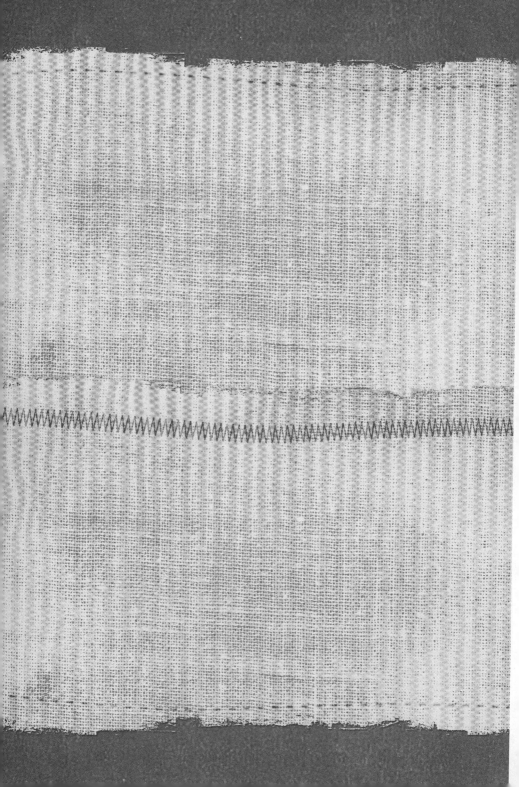

Acknowledgments

When we decided to publish the story of Nonna Lisowskaja Bannister, we didn't realize how our lives—and the way we see the world—would be changed. To know this incredible woman through handwritten notes and photos from her darkest days and then see her survive, meet a remarkable man, marry, and have children can only be possible through her faith in God. We will never forget.

I would particularly like to thank my husband, Dr. Matt Tomlin, who has offered encouragement, support, and love throughout this journey. Special thanks go to my son, Kevin Tomlin, and his wife, Peggy; my daughter, Cindy Tomlin Coulston and her husband, Jimmy; and our six grandchildren.

We feel fortunate in knowing Morris Abernathy, photographer of Union University, Jackson, Tennessee, who offered professional guidance in reproducing the many photos and documents. Special recognition goes to Kathy Bannister, Nonna's daughter-in-law, who helped organize and scan these fragile artifacts.

Thanks to our agent, Greg Johnson, for believing in this book and for offering advice as we pursued this project. We are grateful to Tyndale and the editorial team for their professional advice and willingness to publish this text.

A final thanks to Henry Bannister, who trusted me to know this untold story of his beloved wife, and to his son, John. And to my wonderful friend and coauthor, Denise George, who has made working on this book a joyful experience.

Carolyn R. Tomlin
October 2008

My gratitude goes to all those people whose work, friendship, prayer, and support make a book possible, including my agent, Greg Johnson; Tyndale's wonderful staff; my husband, Dr. Timothy George; my son, Christian George; my daughter, Alyce George; my daughter-in-law, Rebecca Pounds George; and the faculty and staff of Beeson Divinity School, Samford University, Birmingham, Alabama. My special gratitude goes to Henry Bannister and his lovely family for allowing me the unique opportunity of getting to know Nonna through her diaries and photos. And to my good friend and coauthor, Carolyn Tomlin, who invited me into this remarkable project, my greatest thanks!

Denise George
October 2008

About the Editors

Denise George is the author of twenty-four books. She teaches "The Writing Minister" at Beeson Divinity School, Samford University. She is married to Dr. Timothy George. They have two adult children, Christian and Alyce, and one daughter-in-law, Rebecca. They reside in Birmingham, Alabama. You may contact Denise via her Web site, www.authordenisegeorge.com or at her e-mail address, cdwg@aol.com.

Carolyn Tomlin, M.Ed., is a frequent speaker on teaching others to write and publish. She is the author of eight books, writes monthly columns for several magazines and newspapers, and has published more than three thousand articles. Carolyn and her husband, Dr. Matt Tomlin, have two adult children, Cindy and Kevin, and six grandchildren. They reside in Jackson, Tennessee. You may contact Carolyn at her Web site, www.carolyntomlin .com, or via e-mail at carolyn.tomlin@yahoo.com.

Love memoirs?

Find your next great read at MemoirAddict.com!

Memoir ADDICT

At Memoir Addict, we find ordinary people
with extraordinary stories.

Explore:

- updates on new releases
- additional stories from your favorite authors
- FREE first-chapter downloads
- discussion guides
- author videos and book trailers

- inspirational quotes to share on Pinterest, Twitter, and Facebook
- book reviews
- and so much more!

While you're there, check out our blog, featuring unique perspectives on memoirs from all facets of the publishing industry. From authors to acquisition directors to editors, we share our passion for story-telling. You'll get an insider's look at the craft of shaping a story into a captivating memoir.

Are you a memoir addict? Follow us on Twitter @MemoirAddict and on Facebook for updates on your favorite authors, free e-book promotions, contests, and more!

Plus, visit BookClubHub.net to

- download free discussion guides
- get book club recommendations
- sign up for Tyndale's book club and e-newsletters

MemoirAddict.com: ordinary people, extraordinary stories!